W9-CKM-334

Scott Foresman SCIENCE

Series Authors

Dr. Timothy Cooney
Professor of Earth Science and
  Science Education
Earth Science Department
University of Northern Iowa
Cedar Falls, Iowa

Michael Anthony DiSpezio
Science Education Specialist
Cape Cod Children's Museum
Falmouth, Massachusetts

Barbara K. Foots
Science Education Consultant
Houston, Texas

Dr. Angie L. Matamoros
Science Curriculum Specialist
Broward County Schools
Ft. Lauderdale, Florida

Kate Boehm Nyquist
Science Writer and Curriculum Specialist
Mount Pleasant, South Carolina

Dr. Karen L. Ostlund
Professor
Science Education Center
The University of Texas at Austin
Austin, Texas

Contributing Authors

Dr. Anna Uhl Chamot
Associate Professor and
  ESL Faculty Advisor
Department of Teacher Preparation
  and Special Education
Graduate School of Education
  and Human Development
The George Washington University
Washington, D.C.

Dr. Jim Cummins
Professor
Modern Language Centre and
  Curriculum Department
Ontario Institute for Studies in Education
Toronto, Canada

Gale Philips Kahn
Lecturer, Science and Math Education
Elementary Education Department
California State University, Fullerton
Fullerton, California

Vincent Sipkovich
Teacher
Irvine Unified School District
Irvine, California

Steve Weinberg
Science Consultant
Connecticut State
  Department of Education
Hartford, Connecticut

Scott Foresman

Editorial Offices: Glenview, Illinois • Parsippany, New Jersey • New York, New York
Sales Offices: Parsippany, New Jersey • Duluth, Georgia • Glenview, Illinois
Carrollton, Texas • Ontario, California
www.sfscience.com

Content Consultants

Dr. J. Scott Cairns
National Institutes of Health
Bethesda, Maryland

Jackie Cleveland
Elementary Resource Specialist
Mesa Public School District
Mesa, Arizona

Robert L. Kolenda
Science Lead Teacher, K-12
Neshaminy School District
Langhorne, Pennsylvania

David P. Lopath
Teacher
The Consolidated School District
of New Britain
New Britain, Connecticut

Sammantha Lane Magsino
Science Coordinator
Institute of Geophysics
University of Texas at Austin
Austin, Texas

Kathleen Middleton
Director, Health Education
ToucanEd
Soquel, California

Irwin Slesnick
Professor of Biology
Western Washington University
Bellingham, Washington

Dr. James C. Walters
Professor of Geology
University of Northern Iowa
Cedar Falls, Iowa

Multicultural Consultants

Dr. Shirley Gholston Key
Assistant Professor
University of Houston-Downtown
Houston, Texas

Damon L. Mitchell
Quality Auditor
Louisiana-Pacific Corporation
Conroe, Texas

Classroom Reviewers

Kathleen Avery
Teacher
Kellogg Science/Technology Magnet
Wichita, Kansas

Margaret S. Brown
Teacher
Cedar Grove Primary
Williamston, South Carolina

Deborah Browne
Teacher
Whitesville Elementary School
Moncks Corner, South Carolina

Wendy Capron
Teacher
Corlears School
New York, New York

Jiwon Choi
Teacher
Corlears School
New York, New York

John Cirrincione
Teacher
West Seneca Central Schools
West Seneca, New York

Jacqueline Colander
Teacher
Norfolk Public Schools
Norfolk, Virginia

Dr. Terry Contant
Teacher
Conroe Independent
School District
The Woodlands, Texas

Susan Crowley-Walsh
Teacher
Meadowbrook Elementary School
Gladstone, Missouri

Charlene K. Dindo
Teacher
Fairhope K-1 Center/Pelican's Nest
Science Lab
Fairhope, Alabama

Laurie Duffee
Teacher
Barnard Elementary
Tulsa, Oklahoma

Beth Anne Ebler
Teacher
Newark Public Schools
Newark, New Jersey

Karen P. Farrell
Teacher
Rondout Elementary School
District 72
Lake Forest, Illinois

Anna M. Gaiter
Teacher
Los Angeles Unified School District
Los Angeles Systemic Initiative
Los Angeles, California

Federica M. Gallegos
Teacher
Highland Park Elementary
Salt Lake School District
Salt Lake City, Utah

Janet E. Gray
Teacher
Anderson Elementary - Conroe ISD
Conroe, Texas

Karen Guinn
Teacher
Ehrhardt Elementary School - KISD
Spring, Texas

Denis John Hagerty
Teacher
Al Ittihad Private Schools
Dubai, United Arab Emirates

Judith Halpern
Teacher
Bannockburn School
Deerfield, Illinois

Debra D. Harper
Teacher
Community School District 9
Bronx, New York

Gretchen Harr
Teacher
Denver Public Schools - Doull School
Denver, Colorado

Bonnie L. Hawthorne
Teacher
Jim Darcy School
School District 1
Helena, Montana

Marselle Heywood-Julian
Teacher
Community School District 6
New York, New York

Scott Klene
Teacher
Bannockburn School 106
Bannockburn, Illinois

Thomas Kranz
Teacher
Livonia Primary School
Livonia, New York

Tom Leahy
Teacher
Coos Bay School District
Coos Bay, Oregon

Mary Littig
Teacher
Kellogg Science/Technology Magnet
Wichita, Kansas

Patricia Marin
Teacher
Corlears School
New York, New York

Susan Maki
Teacher
Cotton Creek CUSD 118
Island Lake, Illinois

Efraín Meléndez
Teacher
East LA Mathematics Science
Center LAUSD
Los Angeles, California

Becky Mojalid
Teacher
Manarat Jeddah Girls' School
Jeddah, Saudi Arabia

Susan Nations
Teacher
Sulphur Springs Elementary
Tampa, Florida

Brooke Palmer
Teacher
Whitesville Elementary
Moncks Corner, South Carolina

Jayne Pedersen
Teacher
Laura B. Sprague
School District 103
Lincolnshire, Illinois

Shirley Pfingston
Teacher
Orland School District 135
Orland Park, Illinois

Teresa Gayle Rountree
Teacher
Box Elder School District
Brigham City, Utah

Helen C. Smith
Teacher
Schultz Elementary
Klein Independent School District
Tomball, Texas

Denette Smith-Gibson
Teacher
Mitchell Intermediate, CISD
The Woodlands, Texas

Mary Jean Syrek
Teacher
Dr. Charles R. Drew Science
Magnet
Buffalo, New York

Rosemary Troxel
Teacher
Libertyville School District 70
Libertyville, Illinois

Susan D. Vani
Teacher
Laura B. Sprague School
School District 103
Lincolnshire, Illinois

Debra Worman
Teacher
Bryant Elementary
Tulsa, Oklahoma

Dr. Gayla Wright
Teacher
Edmond Public School
Edmond, Oklahoma

# Activity and Safety Consultants

Laura Adams
Teacher
Holley-Navarre Intermediate
Navarre, Florida

Dr. Charlie Ashman
Teacher
Carl Sandburg Middle School
Mundelein District #75
Mundelein, Illinois

Christopher Atlee
Teacher
Horace Mann Elementary
Wichita Public Schools
Wichita, Kansas

David Bachman
Consultant
Chicago, Illinois

Sherry Baldwin
Teacher
Shady Brook
Bedford ISD
Euless, Texas

Pam Bazis
Teacher
Richardson ISD
   Classical Magnet School
Richardson, Texas

Angela Boese
Teacher
McCollom Elementary
Wichita Public Schools USD #259
Wichita, Kansas

Jan Buckelew
Teacher
Taylor Ranch Elementary
Venice, Florida

Shonie Castaneda
Teacher
Carman Elementary, PSJA
Pharr, Texas

Donna Coffey
Teacher
Melrose Elementary - Pinellas
St. Petersburg, Florida

Diamantina Contreras
Teacher
J.T. Brackenridge Elementary
San Antonio ISD
San Antonio, Texas

Susanna Curtis
Teacher
Lake Bluff Middle School
Lake Bluff, Illinois

Karen Farrell
Teacher
Rondout Elementary School,
   Dist. #72
Lake Forest, Illinois

Paul Gannon
Teacher
El Paso ISD
El Paso, Texas

Nancy Garman
Teacher
Jefferson Elementary School
Charleston, Illinois

Susan Graves
Teacher
Beech Elementary
Wichita Public Schools USD #259
Wichita, Kansas

Jo Anna Harrison
Teacher
Cornelius Elementary
Houston ISD
Houston, Texas

Monica Hartman
Teacher
Richard Elementary
Detroit Public Schools
Detroit, Michigan

Kelly Howard
Teacher
Sarasota, Florida

Kelly Kimborough
Teacher
Richardson ISD
   Classical Magnet School
Richardson, Texas

Mary Leveron
Teacher
Velasco Elementary
Brazosport ISD
Freeport, Texas

Becky McClendon
Teacher
A.P. Beutel Elementary
Brazosport ISD
Freeport, Texas

Suzanne Milstead
Teacher
Liestman Elementary
Alief ISD
Houston, Texas

Debbie Oliver
Teacher
School Board of Broward County
Ft. Lauderdale, Florida

Sharon Pearthree
Teacher
School Board of Broward County
Ft. Lauderdale, Florida

Jayne Pedersen
Teacher
Laura B. Sprague School
District 103
Lincolnshire, Illinois

Sharon Pedroja
Teacher
Riverside Cultural
   Arts/History Magnet
Wichita Public Schools USD #259
Wichita, Kansas

Marcia Percell
Teacher
Pharr, San Juan, Alamo ISD
Pharr, Texas

Shirley Pfingston
Teacher
Orland School Dist #135
Orland Park, Illinois

Sharon S. Placko
Teacher
District 26, Mt. Prospect
Mt. Prospect, IL

Glenda Rall
Teacher
Seltzer Elementary
USD #259
Wichita, Kansas

Nelda Requenez
Teacher
Canterbury Elementary
Edinburg, Texas

Dr. Beth Rice
Teacher
Loxahatchee Groves
   Elementary School
Loxahatchee, Florida

Martha Salom Romero
Teacher
El Paso ISD
El Paso, Texas

Paula Sanders
Teacher
Welleby Elementary School
Sunrise, Florida

Lynn Setchell
Teacher
Sigsbee Elementary School
Key West, Florida

Rhonda Shook
Teacher
Mueller Elementary
Wichita Public Schools USD #259
Wichita, Kansas

Anna Marie Smith
Teacher
Orland School Dist. #135
Orland Park, Illinois

Nancy Ann Varneke
Teacher
Seltzer Elementary
Wichita Public Schools USD #259
Wichita, Kansas

Aimee Walsh
Teacher
Rolling Meadows, Illinois

Ilene Wagner
Teacher
O.A. Thorp Scholastic Acacemy
Chicago Public Schools
Chicago, Illinois

Brian Warren
Teacher
Riley Community Consolidated
   School District 18
Marengo, Illinois

Tammie White
Teacher
Holley-Navarre
   Intermediate School
Navarre, Florida

Dr. Mychael Willon
Principal
Horace Mann Elementary
Wichita Public Schools
Wichita, Kansas

Inclusion Consultants

Dr. Eric J. Pyle, Ph.D.
Assistant Professor, Science Education
Department of Educational Theory
   and Practice
West Virginia University
Morgantown, West Virginia

Dr. Gretchen Butera, Ph.D.
Associate Professor, Special Education
Department of Education Theory
   and Practice
West Virginia University
Morgantown, West Virginia

Bilingual Consultant

Irma Gomez-Torres
Dalindo Elementary
Austin ISD
Austin, Texas

Bilingual Reviewers

Mary E. Morales
E.A. Jones Elementary
Fort Bend ISD
Missouri City, Texas

Gabriela T. Nolasco
Pebble Hills Elementary
Ysleta ISD
El Paso, Texas

Maribel B. Tanguma
Reed and Mock Elementary
San Juan, Texas

Yesenia Garza
Reed and Mock Elementary
San Juan, Texas

Teri Gallegos
St. Andrew's School
Austin, Texas

Using Scientific Methods
for Science Inquiry   xii

Using Process Skills
for Science Inquiry   xiv

Science Inquiry   xvi

Unit A
Life Science

Science and Technology   A2

Chapter 1
Structure and
Function of Cells   A4

Explore Activity
Exploring Magnification   A6

Math in Science
Bar Graphs   A7

Lesson 1
**What Are Organisms
Made Of?**   A8

Investigate Activity
Investigating Cells   A14

Lesson 2
**What Are the Parts
of an Animal Cell?**   A16

Lesson 3
**How Do Plant Cells Differ
from Animal Cells?**   A20

Investigate Activity
Investigating Pigments   A24

Lesson 4
How Do Cells Differ?   A26

Experiment Activity
**Experimenting
with Membranes**   A31

Chapter Review   A34

Chapter 2
Reproduction and
Heredity   A36

Explore Activity
**Exploring Variation
in Species**   A38

Math in Science
Metric Conversions   A39

Lesson 1
How Do Cells Reproduce?   A40

Lesson 2
**How Do Many-Celled
Organisms Reproduce?**   A46

Lesson 3
**How Does DNA
Control Traits?**   A52

Investigate Activity
Investigating DNA   A60

Lesson 4
**How Do Organisms
Inherit Traits?**   A62

Investigate Activity
**Investigating Variation
in Seedlings**   A68

Chapter Review   A70

Chapter 3
Changing and Adapting   A72

Explore Activity
Exploring Feeding Adaptations   **A74**

Reading for Science
Drawing Conclusions   **A75**

Lesson 1
What Are Adaptations?   **A76**

Lesson 2
How Do We Know Species Change Over Time?   **A80**

Lesson 3
How Do New Species Evolve?   **A84**

Lesson 4
How Do Organisms Respond to the Environment?   **A92**

Investigate Activity
Observing the Effects of Salt Water on Cells   **A98**

Lesson 5
How Can Behavior Help an Organism Survive?   **A100**

Investigate Activity
Investigating How Plants React to Light   **A106**

Chapter Review   **A108**

Chapter 4
Ecosystems and Biomes   A110

Explore Activity
Exploring a Water Ecosystem   **A112**

Reading for Science
Making Predictions   **A113**

Lesson 1
How Do Organisms Interact?   **A114**

Investigate Activity
Observing a Bottle Ecosystem   **A122**

Lesson 2
How Are Materials Recycled?   **A124**

Lesson 3
What Happens When an Ecosystem Changes?   **A130**

Lesson 4
What Are the Features of Land Biomes?   **A136**

Investigate Activity
Investigating Soils   **A146**

Lesson 5
What Are the Features of Water Biomes?   **A148**

Chapter Review   **A154**

Unit A Review   **A156**

Unit A Performance Review   **A158**

Writing for Science   **A160**

Go to EARTH SCIENCE UNIT C Table of Contents

Unit B
Physical Science

Science and Technology   **B2**

Chapter 1
Heat and Matter   B4

Explore Activity
Exploring Temperature Scales   **B6**

Math in Science
Positive and Negative Numbers   **B7**

Lesson 1
What Is Heat?   **B8**

Lesson 2
How Does Heat Affect Matter?   **B14**

Investigate Activity
Comparing Expansion and Contraction   **B18**

Lesson 3
How Can Matter Become Heated?   **B20**

Investigate Activity
Keeping Ice Frozen   **B26**

Chapter Review   **B28**

Chapter 2
Changes in Matter   B30

Explore Activity
Exploring Dissolving   **B32**

Reading for Science
Using Context Tools   **B33**

Lesson 1
How Does Matter Change State?   **B34**

Lesson 2
How Do Solutions Form?   **B40**

Investigate Activity
Investigating Solutions   **B48**

Lesson 3
How Are Chemical Reactions Described?   **B50**

Investigate Activity
Investigating Temperature Change in a Reaction   **B60**

Lesson 4
What Are the Properties of Acids and Bases?   **B62**

Experiment Activity
Experimenting with Acids and Bases   **B69**

Chapter Review   **B72**

Chapter 3
Moving Objects   B 74

Explore Activity
Exploring Acceleration   B 76

Reading for Science
**Identifying Cause
and Effect   B 77**

Lesson 1
**What Causes Objects
to Move or Stop Moving?   B 78**

Lesson 2
How Is Motion Described?   B 86

Lesson 3
**What Is Newton's
First Law of Motion?   B 94**

Investigate Activity
**Investigating Friction
and Motion   B 100**

Lesson 4
**What Is Newton's
Second Law of Motion?   B 102**

Lesson 5
**What Is Newton's
Third Law of Motion?   B 106**

Investigate Activity
**Investigating Action
and Reaction   B 110**

Chapter Review   B 112

Chapter 4
Light, Color
and Sound   B 114

Explore Activity
Exploring Light Rays   B 116

Math in Science
Measuring Angles   B 117

Lesson 1
What Is Light?   B 118

Lesson 2
How Does Light Behave?   B 122

Investigate Activity
Investigating Light   B 130

Lesson 3
What Is Color?   B 132

Lesson 4
What Is Sound?   B 140

Investigate Activity
**Investigating
Sound Insulation   B 152**

Chapter Review   B 154

Unit B Review   B 156

Unit B Performance Review   B 158

Writing for Science   B 160

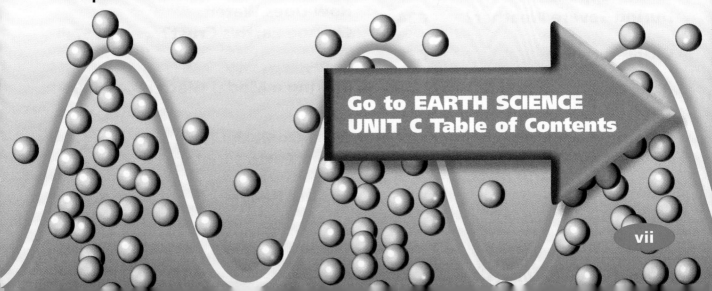

Go to EARTH SCIENCE
UNIT C Table of Contents

Unit C

Earth Science

Here is the
Table of
Contents

Science and Technology C2

Chapter 1
Technology and Weather C4

Explore Activity
Exploring Weather Patterns C6

Math in Science
Percent C7

Lesson 1
How Do Weather and Technology Affect People? C8

Lesson 2
What Interactions Determine Weather? C11

Lesson 3
How Is Technology Used to Collect Weather Data? C18

Investigate Activity
Measuring Relative Humidity C26

Lesson 4
How Are Weather Forecasts Made? C28

Lesson 5
What Happens During Severe Weather? C34

Chapter Review C38

Chapter 2
Earth Processes C40

Explore Activity
Exploring Properties of the Earth's Mantle C42

Reading for Science
Using Graphic Sources C43

Lesson 1
What Changes Occur Within Earth's Crust? C44

Investigate Activity
Making a Model Seismograph C52

Lesson 2
How Does Soil Form? C54

Lesson 3
How Does Water Change Earth's Crust? C57

Investigate Activity
Making a Model Glacier C66

Lesson 4
What Do Rocks Tell About Earth's History?

Chapter Review C76

Chapter 3
Exploring the Universe
C78

Explore Activity
Exploring Lunar Eclipses   C80

Math in Science
Using Large Numbers   C81

Lesson 1
What Is Earth's Place in Space?   C82

Lesson 2
What Do We Know About the Sun?   C87

Lesson 3
What Makes Up the Universe?   C91

Investigate Activity
Making a Model of the Expanding Universe   C98

Lesson 4
How Do People Explore Space?   C100

Chapter Review   C106

Chapter 4
Resources and Conservation
C108

Explore Activity
Exploring Recycling   C110

Reading for Science
Comparing and Contrasting   C111

Lesson 1
How Do People Affect Earth's Resources?   C112

Lesson 2
What Resources Do Air and Land Provide?   C115

Lesson 3
What Resources Does Water Provide?   C119

Investigate Activity
Purifying Water   C126

Lesson 4
How Can You Be a Good Steward of Earth's Resources?   C128

Experiment Activity
Experimenting with Erosion Control   C135

Chapter Review   C138

Unit C Review   C140

Unit C Performance Review   C142

Writing for Science   C144

Unit D
Human Body

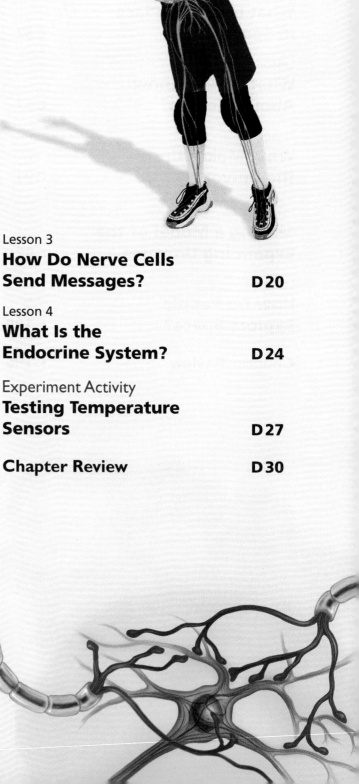

Science and Technology   **D 2**

Chapter 1
**Your Body's
Control Systems**   **D 4**

Explore Activity
Exploring Reaction Time   **D 6**

Math in Science
Rate   **D 7**

Lesson 1
**What Is the
Nervous System?**   **D 8**

Lesson 2
**How Do Your Senses
Gather Information?**   **D 14**

Investigate Activity
Investigating Vision   **D 18**

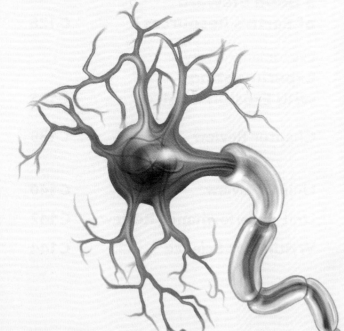

Lesson 3
**How Do Nerve Cells
Send Messages?**   **D 20**

Lesson 4
**What Is the
Endocrine System?**   **D 24**

Experiment Activity
**Testing Temperature
Sensors**   **D 27**

Chapter Review   **D 30**

Chapter 2
Drugs and Your Body D 32

Explore Activity
Exploring Healthful Habits D 34

Reading for Science
Supporting Facts and Details D 35

Lesson 1
What Should You Know About Drugs? D 36

Investigate Activity
Observing Particle Distribution D 42

Lesson 2
How Does Tobacco Affect Your Body? D 44

Lesson 3
What Are the Dangers of Marijuana Use? D 50

Lesson 4
How Does Alcohol Harm Your Body? D 52

Chapter Review D 58

Unit D Review D 60

Unit D Performance Review D 62

Writing for Science D 64

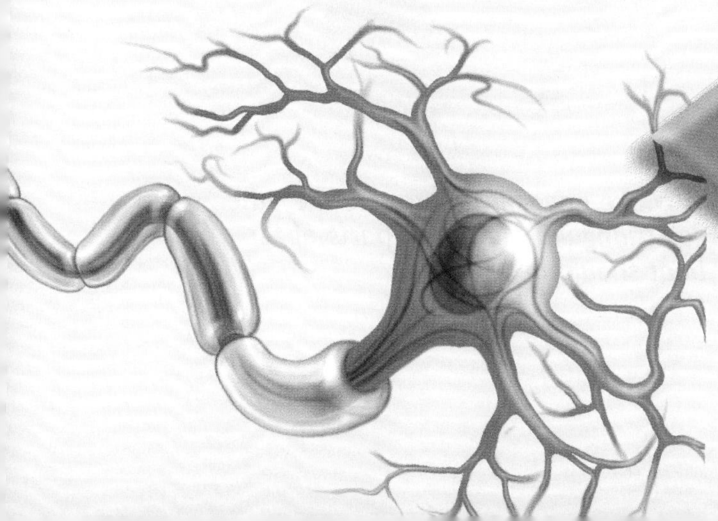

Your Science Handbook

Table of Contents 1

⚠️ **Safety in Science** 2

Using the Metric System 4

Science Process Skill Lessons
Observing 6
Communicating 8
Classifying 10
Estimating and Measuring 12
Inferring 14
Predicting 16
Making Operational Definitions 18
Making and Using Models 20
Formulating Questions and Hypotheses 22
Collecting and Interpreting Data 24
Identifying and Controlling Variables 26
Experimenting 28

Science Reference Section 30

History of Science 44

Ⓗ **Glossary** 56

Index 65

Go to EARTH SCIENCE
UNIT C Table of Contents

Using Scientific Methods for Science Inquiry

Scientists try to solve many problems. Scientists study problems in different ways, but they all use scientific methods to guide their work. Scientific methods are organized ways of finding answers and solving problems. Scientific methods include the steps shown on these pages. The order of the steps or the number of steps used may change. You can use these steps to organize your own scientific inquiries.

State the Problem

The problem is the question you want to answer. Curiosity and inquiry have resulted in many scientific discoveries. State your problem in the form of a question.

Which sail design makes a boat move faster?

Formulate Your Hypothesis

Your hypothesis is a possible answer to your problem. Make sure your hypothesis can be tested. Your hypothesis should take the form of a statement.

◀ *A square sail will make a boat move faster.*

Identify and Control the Variables

For a fair test, you must select which variable to change and which variables to control. Choose one variable to change when you test your hypothesis. Control the other variables so they do not change.

▲ *Make one sail square and the other sail triangular. The other parts of the boat should be the same.*

Test Your Hypothesis

Do experiments to test your hypothesis. You may need to repeat experiments to make sure your results remain consistent. Sometimes you conduct a scientific survey to test a hypothesis.

◀ Place the boat in the water. Use a straw to blow air onto the sail for 10 seconds. Measure how far the boat goes. Repeat with the other boat.

Collect Your Data

As you test your hypothesis, you will collect data about the problem you want to solve. You may need to record measurements. You might make drawings or diagrams. Or you may write lists or descriptions. Collect as much data as you can while testing your hypothesis.

Distance boat moved	
Square sail	43 cm
Triangular sail	26 cm

Interpret Your Data

By organizing your data into charts, tables, diagrams, and graphs, you may see patterns in the data. Then you can decide what the information from your data means.

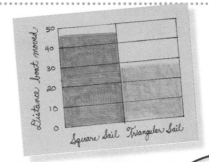

State Your Conclusion

Your conclusion is a decision you make based on evidence. Compare your results with your hypothesis. Based on whether or not your data supports your hypothesis, decide if your hypothesis is correct or incorrect. Then communicate your conclusion by stating or presenting your decision.

The square sail moves the boat faster.

Inquire Further

Use what you learn to solve other problems or to answer other questions that you might have. You may decide to repeat your experiment, or to change it based on what you learned.

◀ Does the shape of the boat affect its speed?

Using Process Skills for Science Inquiry

These 12 process skills are used by scientists when they do their research. You also use many of these skills every day. For example, when you think of a statement that you can test, you are using process skills. When you gather data to make a chart or graph, you are using process skills. As you do the activities in your book, you will use these same process skills.

Observing

Use one or more of your senses—seeing, hearing, smelling, touching, or tasting—to gather information about objects or events.

I see..., I smell..., I hear..., It feels like..., I never taste without permission!

Communicating

Share information about what you learn using words, pictures, charts, graphs, and diagrams.

Classifying

Arrange or group objects according to their common properties.

◀ *Shells with one color in Group 1.*

Shells with two or more colors in Group 2. ▶

Estimating and Measuring

Make an estimate about an object's properties, then measure and describe the object in units.

I think what's in here is shaped like . . .

Inferring

Draw a conclusion or make a reasonable guess based on what you observe, or from your past experiences.

Predicting

Form an idea about what will happen based on evidence.

◀ *Predict what type of sail will work best.*

An acid is a substance that changes blue litmus paper to... ▶

Making Operational Definitions

Define or describe an object or event based on your experiences with it.

Making and Using Models

Make real or mental representations to explain ideas, objects, or events.

◀ *My model mouth is like a real mouth because...*

If I add another washer... ▶

Formulating Questions and Hypotheses

Think of a statement that you can test to solve a problem or to answer a question about how something works.

Collecting and Interpreting Data

Gather observations and measurements into graphs, tables, charts, or diagrams. Then use the information to solve problems or answer questions.

Adding salt to water raises the boiling point of the water.

Change	Same
⮑ Height of ramp	⮑ Length of ramp
	⮑ Ramp surface
	⮑ car

Identifying and Controlling Variables

Change one factor that may affect the outcome of an event while holding other factors constant.

I'll write a clear procedure so that other students could repeat the experiment.

Experimenting

Design an investigation to test a hypothesis or to solve a problem. Then form a conclusion.

? Science Inquiry

Throughout your science book, you will ask questions, do investigations, answer your questions, and tell others what you have learned. Use the descriptions below to help you during your scientific inquiries.

1 Ask questions that can be answered by scientific investigations.
Direct your questions and inquiries toward objects and events that can be described, explained, or predicted by scientific investigations.

2 Design and conduct a scientific investigation.
Investigations can include using scientific methods to carry out science inquiry. As you conduct your investigations, you will relate your ideas to current scientific knowledge, suggest alternate explanations, and evaluate explanations and procedures.

3 Use appropriate tools, and methods to gather, analyze, and interpret data.
The tools and methods you use will depend on the questions you ask and the investigations you design. A computer can be a useful tool for collecting, summarizing, and displaying your data.

4 Use data to develop descriptions, suggest explanations, make predictions, and construct models.
Base your explanations and descriptions on the information that you have gathered. In addition, understanding scientific subject matter will help you develop explanations, identify causes, and recognize relationships of events you observe with science content.

5 Use logic to make relationships between data and explanations.
Review and summarize the data you have gathered in your investigation. Use logic to determine the cause and effect relationships in the events and variables you observe.

6 Analyze alternative explanations and predictions.
Listen to, consider, and evaluate explanations offered by others. Asking questions and querying and evaluating explanations is part of scientific inquiry.

7 Communicate procedures and explanations.
Share your investigations with others by describing your methods, observations, results, and explanations.

8 Use mathematics to analyze data and construct explanations.
Use mathematics in your investigations to gather, organize, and collect data and to present explanations and results in a meaningful manner.

Unit C
Earth Science

Chapter 1
Technology and Weather   C 4

Chapter 2
Earth Processes   C 40

Chapter 3
Exploring the Universe   C 78

Chapter 4
Resources and Conservation   C 108

Your Science Handbook

Table of Contents   1

Safety in Science   2

Using the Metric System   4

Science Process Skills Lessons   6

Science Reference Section   30

History of Science   44

Glossary   56

Index   65

Science and Technology
In Your World!

Weather? Or Not?

Putting your hand out the window to tell if it's raining is a thing of the past. Today, TV and the Internet show radar images of approaching tornadoes or storms. You can even carry a device that tells when thunder and lightning are coming. Learn about weather forecasting in **Chapter 1 Technology and Weather.**

Exploring Earth's Deep Water

Oceans cover about 70 percent of Earth. New manned submarines that can stand up to extreme pressures are helping to solve the mysteries of the deep. Hundreds of unknown species and mineral-rich hot-water vents on the ocean floors have been discovered. Learn more about Earth's oceans in **Chapter 2 Earth Processes.**

Earthly Uses for Moon Tools

Did you know that cordless tools were first developed to help Apollo astronauts dig into the moon? And Lunar Rover controls can enable paraplegics to drive cars? Find out about space exploration and more in **Chapter 3 Exploring the Universe.**

Metal Munching Microbes

Mining metal ores and refining them has long harmed the environment. Scientists, however, have found microbes that can simply "chew up" the rock and—PRESTO! Mine wastes are gone and even more metal remains. Learn about resources and protecting the environment in **Chapter 4 Resources and Conservation.**

Grab Your Umbrella!

The radar weather map shows that heavy rains are on their way. What other technology do weather scientists use to predict the weather?

Chapter 1
Technology and Weather

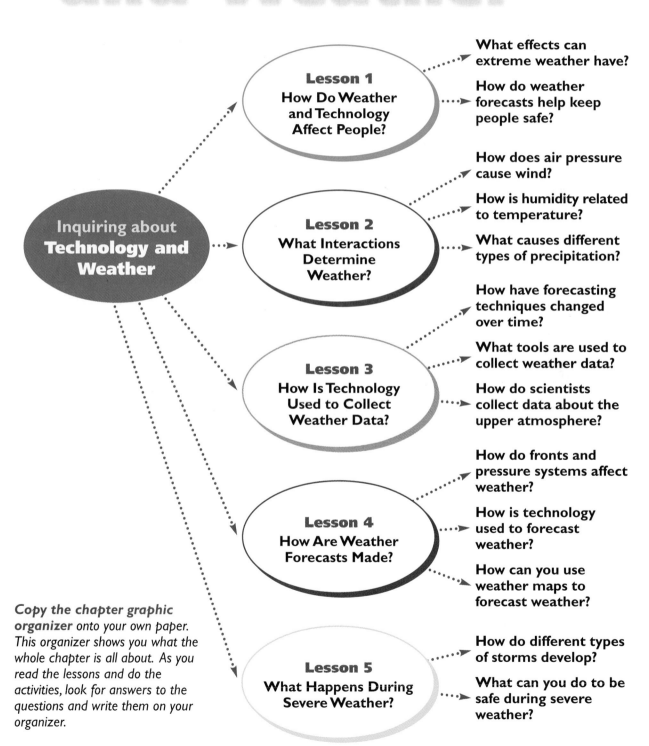

Lesson 1
How Do Weather and Technology Affect People?

What effects can extreme weather have?

How do weather forecasts help keep people safe?

Inquiring about Technology and Weather

Lesson 2
What Interactions Determine Weather?

How does air pressure cause wind?

How is humidity related to temperature?

What causes different types of precipitation?

Lesson 3
How Is Technology Used to Collect Weather Data?

How have forecasting techniques changed over time?

What tools are used to collect weather data?

How do scientists collect data about the upper atmosphere?

Lesson 4
How Are Weather Forecasts Made?

How do fronts and pressure systems affect weather?

How is technology used to forecast weather?

How can you use weather maps to forecast weather?

Lesson 5
What Happens During Severe Weather?

How do different types of storms develop?

What can you do to be safe during severe weather?

Copy the chapter graphic organizer onto your own paper. This organizer shows you what the whole chapter is all about. As you read the lessons and do the activities, look for answers to the questions and write them on your organizer.

C5

Exploring Weather Patterns

Process Skills

- observing
- communicating

Materials

- weather reports

Explore

1 Obtain newspaper weather reports for one week. Arrange the reports in the order of their dates, with the earliest date first, as shown in the photo.

2 Observe the symbols on the map in each weather report. Look at each type of symbol you see on the maps. Notice the location of the symbols on each map. Observe how the position of the symbols on the map changes from day to day.

3 Look at the weather report for Day 1 and record the weather prediction for Day 2. Next, find out the actual weather for Day 2. This data may be in the report for Day 2 or Day 3. Record the actual weather for Day 2.

4 Repeat step 3 for a total of 5 days.

Reflect

1. What kinds of symbols did the weather reports show?

2. How did the location of the symbols change?

3. Communicate. Discuss with others in your group how you think weather forecasters use those patterns to help make predictions about the weather.

? Inquire Further

What other kinds of data do you think can help predict the weather? Develop a plan to answer this or other questions you may have.

Percent

How often do you think your local weather forecaster is accurate? You can express this quantity as a **percent**. For example, you might say that your local weather forecaster is right 85% of the time.

A percent is a ratio that compares a part to a whole using the number 100. The percent is the number of hundredths that represent the part.

Math Vocabulary

percent, a ratio comparing a part to a whole using the number 100; the percent is the number of hundredths that the part is equal to

Example

Relative humidity is a ratio of the amount of water vapor in the air to how much water vapor the air can hold at that temperature. This ratio can be expressed as a percent. The grid represents the total amount of water vapor that air can hold at a given temperature. The shaded region represents the amount of water vapor that is actually present at a certain time. What is the relative humidity in the air?

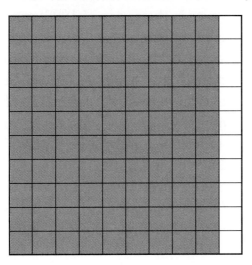

Each shaded section is $\frac{1}{100}$ of the figure. Ninety squares, or $\frac{90}{100}$, are shaded. So, because $\frac{90}{100} = 0.90$, the relative humidity is 90%.

Talk About It!

1. What is 100% of something? What is 0% of something?

2. Write 86% as a fraction.

You will learn:

- what effects extreme weather can have.
- how weather forecasts help keep people safe.

Lesson 1

How Do Weather and Technology Affect People?

Hiss! Crackle! Sizzle! The sound of fire can be pleasing when it's in a fireplace or campfire. However, when the fire is out of control, burning brush and trees in its path, and heading for your home—well, how would you feel? What would you do?

Extreme Weather

Florida, you may know, is famous for its warm, wet climate. However, in the spring of 1998, that warmth became extreme. In May, a heat wave began that stretched into June. In one Florida town, the temperature was above 35°C more than 20 days in a row. Yet while the warmth increased, the usual wetness decreased. The late-spring rains that commonly fall in the state never came. The combination of heat and drought began to affect life in the place called the Sunshine State.

At first, the effects were not too unusual. People planned fewer outdoor activities. They used more and more water. Government officials alerted them to the health threat posed by extreme heat.

Then, over the Memorial Day weekend, an even greater threat flared up—wildfire! The drought had made the Florida pine forests and brush dry and easy to burn. Lightning from brief storms started wildfires that quickly raged across the state. The map and photo on the next page show how many wildfires there were and how widely the fires spread.

This map shows that thousands of wildfires burned in Florida in early summer, 1998. Most occurred in the northeastern part of the state. ▼

Tallahassee Lake City Jacksonville Daytona Beach Orlando Melbourne Miami

- ☐ No reported fires
- ☐ 1 to 100 fires
- ☐ 101 to 1,000 fires
- ☐ 1,001 to 5,000 fires
- ☐ Greater than 5,000 fires
- • Most serious fires
- —— 100 km

Weather Forecasts Keep People Safe

Why couldn't firefighters stop the fires? Wildfires in Florida happen every year. However, tropical storms usually help put them out. In June and early July of 1998, the people of Florida waited for those storms, but the storms didn't come. Instead, dry northwest winds blew the fires from treetop to treetop and over highways and firebreaks made by firefighters. The fires continued to burn.

While wind can help spread a fire, rain can help put it out. Therefore, as the Florida fires burned, weather data became extremely important. Firefighters, like the one in the photo, especially needed accurate information about wind direction and speed. Their lives—and the lives of people in the fire's path—depended on it.

That's where **meteorologists**—scientists who study the weather—came in. Meteorologists use weather instruments to collect data about the weather. Such data include temperature, wind speed, wind direction, precipitation, and air pressure. Then meteorologists use the data and their knowledge of weather patterns to **forecast**, or predict, what the weather will be.

Meteorologists from the National Weather Service work closely with firefighters when wildfires break out. Incident Meteorologists (IMETs) go directly to the site of the fire. They take with them movable forecasting equipment and laptop computers. With this technology, the IMETs prepare up-to-date "microscale" forecasts— weather predictions for the exact spot where the fire is burning. They look for weather conditions that may endanger firefighters. Then the IMETs inform fire-control management teams so that they know where firefighting crews can safely go.

meteorologist (mē′tē ə rol′ə jist), scientist who studies the weather

forecast (fôr′kast′), a prediction of what the weather will be like in the near future

Firefighters risked their lives but could not stop the Florida fires. This weather satellite image shows smoke rising from the Florida fires. ▼

C9

Forecasts aren't always correct. When your local weather forecaster is wrong, what might happen to you? Perhaps you'll get caught in the rain without an umbrella. When the weather forecast for a fire-management team is wrong, people can lose their lives. Property such as homes and stores can be destroyed. Valuable natural resources such as forests can burn. Improving the science of weather forecasting is an important ongoing goal.

The IMETs who came to Florida worked to predict where the fires would be blown by the wind. People in neighborhoods, in towns, even in whole counties were ordered to evacuate when fires were predicted to move into their area. Emergency relief workers helped.

By the middle of July, scattered showers and east winds off the ocean began to stop the spread of the wildfires. Firefighters were able to get most fires under control. At least 350 homes had been damaged or destroyed. You can see one of them below. However, because of the work of meteorologists, firefighters, and others, not one person had been killed or seriously hurt.

The owner of this house was evacuated safely but lost his home in a Florida wildfire. ▼

Lesson 1 Review

1. What are some effects that extreme weather can have?

2. How do weather forecasts help keep people safe?

3. **Cause and Effect**
   What were two causes of the fires in Florida in the Spring of 1998?

What Interactions Determine Weather?

SWOOSH! Hold on to your hat! That breeze is brisk, and it may be signaling a change in the weather. Wind is a funny thing. You can't see it, or draw it, or take a photograph of it—but you sure can feel it.

You will learn:
- how air pressure causes wind.
- how temperature and humidity are related.
- what causes different types of precipitation.

Air Pressure and Wind

Where does weather happen? It happens in the air around you. What's going on in that air to cause weather? Plenty. Gas particles in the air are in constant motion. They are pushing against each other and against the ground. Right now the air around you has a certain temperature and some amount of moisture. The air might contain clouds, or rain, or snow. All of these conditions of the air are interacting with each other to make the weather you're experiencing.

Physical Science One of the air conditions that affects weather is air pressure. Gas particles in the air are matter and have mass. The force of gravity pulls on this mass, which causes the gases to push against Earth's surface. This push is called **air pressure.** You can think of air pressure as the weight of air. You usually don't feel air pressure because the air inside you pushes out with the same force as the air outside you pushes in.

So, what does air pressure have to do with weather? The picture to the right gives you a clue. When air is heated, its molecules move faster and farther apart. The air becomes less dense, and, therefore, the air pressure lowers. A region with low pressure is called a low. As air cools, the molecules slow down and move closer together. The air becomes denser and pushes with greater pressure. A region of high pressure is a high.

Glossary

air pressure
(er presh′ər), the force of air against Earth's surface

Glossary

High Pressure   **Low Pressure**

▲ *Which of these columns of air represents colder air? What do you think happens between the region of high pressure and the region of low pressure?*

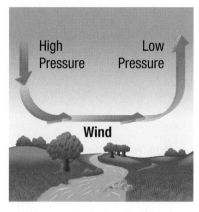

▲ Wind results when air moves from regions of high pressure to regions of low pressure.

Are you still wondering how air pressure affects the weather? Remember that molecules in the warm air of a low are farther apart than in the surrounding air. This means that warm air is less dense than an equal volume of cooler air. Because warm air is less dense, it tends to rise from the earth's surface.

Like other gases, air moves from a region of higher density to a region of lower density. As shown in the picture to the left, the cold, high-pressure air moves in to replace the rising air. You can't see this process, but you have felt it many times. This air moving from high- to low-pressure areas is called wind. When the differences in air pressure are great, watch out! You can expect strong winds. When the differences in air pressure are small, you can enjoy gentle breezes.

Temperature and Humidity

When you step outside in the afternoon, the air temperature may be the first weather condition you notice. If the sun has warmed the air to 32°C, you might feel uncomfortably hot. A cloudy day might be a bit cooler because the clouds block some of the sun's energy. At higher altitudes, such as in the mountains, it might be cooler too. Here, the air is less dense and there are fewer air molecules to absorb the sun's energy.

Water evaporates when it changes from a liquid to a gas. As sweat evaporates, it uses some of your body's energy and you feel cooler. However, evaporation occurs slowly when humid air already holds all the water vapor it can possibly hold. ▼

The girl in the picture is certainly noticing the air temperature. She's noticing another weather condition too. Can you guess what it is? At times the weather feels hot and sticky. Perspiration drips down your face even if you're not running or working hard. That's when people say, "It's not the heat. It's the humidity."

Humidity is moisture in the air in the form of a gas called water vapor. This water vapor comes from oceans, lakes, rainfall, and other sources from which water evaporates into the air.

Sometimes the air has more water vapor than at other times. The amount of water vapor that air can hold depends largely on the air temperature. Imagine you have a container like the one to the right. Notice that the warmer the temperature, the more water vapor the container can hold. Lower the temperature, and you lower the amount of water vapor the air can hold.

Meteorologists refer to relative humidity when reporting how much water vapor is in the air. **Relative humidity** is a ratio that compares the amount of water vapor in the air to the largest amount of moisture the air can hold at that temperature. A 65 percent relative humidity means the air is holding 65 percent of the water vapor it can hold at that temperature. If the temperature increases, would the relative humidity increase, decrease, or stay the same? Why?

Once air has reached 100 percent relative humidity, it can't hold any more water vapor. At this point, water vapor condenses, or returns to its liquid form. The temperature at which water vapor condenses is called a **dew point.** The water droplets on the plant in the picture formed when the cooler night air reached its dew point.

Have you noticed that grass and flowers are often wet in the early morning, even if it has not rained? Drops of dew form when water vapor condenses out of the cool night air. ▼

Glossary

humidity (hyü mid′ə tē), water vapor in the air

relative humidity (rel′ə tiv hyü mid′ə tē), measurement that compares the amount of water vapor in air with the amount the air can hold at a certain temperature

dew point (dü point), the temperature at which a volume of air cannot hold any more water vapor

24°C   10°C

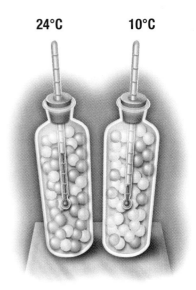

▲ *Warmer air can hold more water vapor than the same volume of cooler air.*

C13

Clouds and Precipitation

Have you seen any water in the air today? If there are clouds in the sky, you could answer "yes." That's mostly what clouds are—water.

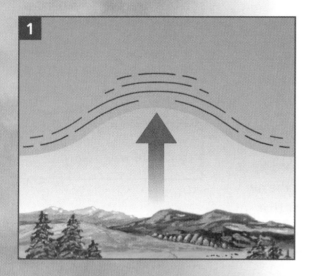

To understand how clouds form, remember how changes in temperature affect humidity. Then think of this example. It is a clear spring day. Throughout the day, the sun warms the ground, which in turn warms the air. This warm air holds a certain amount of water vapor. The warm air rises and cools, as in the first drawing to the left. At the cooler temperature, the air can no longer hold that much water vapor. The "extra" water vapor condenses onto microscopic particles of salt and dust in the air. Tiny water droplets form. They are so small and light that they float in the air. Collections of millions of these droplets form clouds. Because the temperature in clouds can be below freezing, even in the summer, some of the water vapor turns into tiny ice crystals.

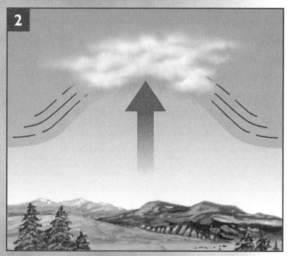

Did you ever try to find different shapes in clouds? As clouds move in the wind and evaporate, they may take on the shape of anything you can imagine. However, clouds can be classified into a few basic kinds with a few basic shapes. The names of clouds give a clue to their appearance. For example, the term *strato* means "sheetlike," *cirro* means "curl," *nimbo* means "rain," and *cumulo* means "pile or heap." The types of clouds are grouped according to their height above the ground. You can see the four basic types of clouds on the next page.

Forming Clouds

◀ (1) The sun heats the ground, sending up columns of air where the ground is warmest. (2) If the air is moist enough, clouds form when the rising air cools to its dew point. (3) The clouds grow as rising moist air continues to condense into millions of tiny water droplets and ice crystals.

Classification of Clouds

Low Clouds

Low clouds such as stratus clouds are usually seen as smooth, even sheets. They may appear as a thick, gray blanket that can bring drizzle, rain, or snow.

Middle Clouds

Middle clouds include altocumulus clouds, which can appear as small patches arranged in bands across the sky or in irregular groups.

High Clouds

High clouds like these cirrus clouds are the delicate, wispy clouds with curled edges that appear in the sky at high altitudes. Cirrus clouds are so high and cold that they are made completely of ice crystals.

Vertical Clouds

Vertical clouds appear at more than one height. An example is the cumulonimbus cloud that rises to great heights while its base is near the ground. These clouds often produce thunderstorms.

It is probably no surprise to you that clouds are associated with precipitation such as rain and snow. However, it may surprise you to learn that most rain that falls in the United States begins as snow. Ice crystals that are high in the clouds grow when more and more water vapor condenses on them. Eventually, they become so heavy that they start to fall. As the ice crystals fall through a cloud, they may collide and combine with other ice crystals or water droplets. When the crystals become too heavy to float in the air, they fall as precipitation.

The pictures below, and on the next page, show what happens to ice crystals when they fall through bands of air at different temperatures. If the air remains cold, the crystals reach the ground as snow. If the ice crystals fall far enough through air that is warm, the crystals melt and reach the ground as rain.

Sometimes rain briefly passes through a band of colder air just before reaching the ground. The water droplets freeze the moment they hit something. This precipitation is called freezing rain. It can be dangerous because it glazes roads and sidewalks with ice.

Types of Precipitation

Most precipitation in the United States starts as ice crystals. The kind of precipitation that reaches the ground depends on the temperature of the air through which it falls. ▼

Snow falls into cold air and never melts.

Snow

Snow falls from clouds and melts into rain in the warm air.

Rain

Sleet forms when the ice crystals melt into raindrops but refreeze during a long journey through cold air. The frozen raindrops of sleet can sting when they hit your uncovered skin. The photo shows an unusual kind of precipitation—hail. These pellets of ice form as air currents toss ice crystals up and down within a cumulonimbus cloud. Water collects on the crystal as it falls through the cloud and freezes on the crystal as it rises higher in the cloud. The hailstone grows in this way until it becomes too heavy for the air to hold up and falls to the ground. Which kind of precipitation has most recently fallen where you live?

Lesson 2 Review

1. What causes wind?

2. How is temperature related to humidity?

3. How do different types of precipitation form?

4. **Percent**
   The relative humidity at a particular location on Day 1 is 60 percent. On Day 2 it is 75 percent. On which day does the air hold more water vapor?

▲ Hail sometimes falls during a powerful thunderstorm. Hailstones may be as small as a sand grain or as large as a baseball.

Snow melts in warm air, . . .

. . . cools before freezing in cold air, and becomes ice when it hits the ground.

Freezing Rain

Snow melts in warm air, . . .

. . . and refreezes into sleet in cold air.

Sleet

You will learn:

- how forecasting technologies have changed over time.
- what tools are currently used to collect weather data.
- how scientists collect data about the upper atmosphere.

People's desire and need to understand the weather is as old as civilization itself. Ancient Babylonians recorded weather data on these clay tablets. ▼

Lesson 3

How Is Technology Used to Collect Weather Data?

"Sea gull, sea gull, sit on the sand. It's a sign of a rain when you are at hand." What does that mean?! This rhyme is one of the many rules of thumb people once used to help predict the weather. Is there any truth to it? How did forecasting get from rhymes to where we are today?

History of Forecasting

History of Science

The ancient Babylonians were among the first people who tried to forecast weather. They observed nature and recorded on clay tablets thousands of omens, or signs, about the weather. Two of these tablets are shown in the picture.

One of the earliest-known weather instruments was a wind vane used in ancient Rome. This type of instrument is still a useful tool for determining wind direction.

The ancient Greeks were also involved in early forecasting. In fact, the word *meteorology* comes from a Greek term, *meteora,* which means "things in the air." Aristotle, a philosopher of ancient Greece, wrote a book about weather in 340 B.C. His ideas were based on his observations of the sky.

People sometimes created weather sayings, or proverbs, based on observations they made. Farmers and sailors especially used these proverbs and passed them down through the ages. Look at a small sampling of such proverbs on the next page. Some of them were fairly reliable, especially those that refer to conditions of the air such as clouds, winds, or the sky.

In the 1500s and 1600s, many instruments were invented to measure weather conditions. For example, an Italian scientist named Galileo Galilei invented a thermometer in 1593. About 50 years later, a student of Galileo's named Evangelista Torricelli invented a **barometer.** This instrument measures air pressure. As the picture shows, Torricelli's barometer consisted of a dish of mercury and a glass tube. Air pushing down on the mercury in the dish holds the column of mercury in the tube at a certain height. As the pressure on the mercury in the dish changes, the height of the column changes. Scientists used these new instruments along with their knowledge about matter and motion to speculate about the weather.

The development of weather technology continued. In 1837, an American inventor, Samuel F. B. Morse, perfected the telegraph. This technology enabled meteorologists to quickly share their weather observations from one place to another, and warn people of approaching storms. Eventually, weather information was being shared among weather services of different countries. The United States established its own Weather Bureau in 1890.

Glossary

barometer
(bə rom′ə tər), an instrument used to measure air pressure

Proverbs

Sea gull, sea gull, sit on the sand. It's a sign of a rain when you are at hand.

Red sky at night, sailor's delight, red sky in morning, sailors take warning.

Frogs croak before a rain, but in the sun stay quiet again.

The higher the clouds, the better the weather.

▲ Do you think any of these proverbs have scientific truth? Write some of your own weather proverbs.

◀ Torricelli proved Galileo's finding that air had weight when he built this simple barometer in 1643.

Glossary

anemometer
(an′ə mom′ə tər), an instrument used to measure wind speed

psychrometer
(sī krom′ə tər), an instrument used to measure relative humidity

Collecting Weather Data

Watching the weather can be anything but dull! To keep track of all the factors that make up the weather, you need to measure changes in conditions such as temperature, wind speed, humidity, and air pressure. What tools can you use to do this?

Anemometer

◀ This hand-held, high-tech *anemometer* measures wind speed. It's a modern version of the instrument that Leonardo da Vinci invented more than 500 years ago. The cups catch the wind and spin, turning a dial that measures wind speed. You can estimate wind speed too. Just look out the window and compare what you see with this chart.

Wind Speed	
km/h	**Evidence of Speed**
Less than 1	Calm; smoke rises straight up
2–5	Smoke moves in direction of wind
6–12	Wind felt on face; leaves rustle
13–20	Leaves and small twigs move
21–29	Dust and loose paper move
30–39	Small trees move
40–50	Large branches move
51–60	Large trees move

Psychrometer

A **psychrometer** is an instrument that uses two thermometers to measure relative humidity. Notice that a wet cloth covers the bulb on one of the thermometers. Water evaporates from this cloth, lowering the temperature on that thermometer. Relative humidity is found by comparing the two different temperatures on a special chart. ▶

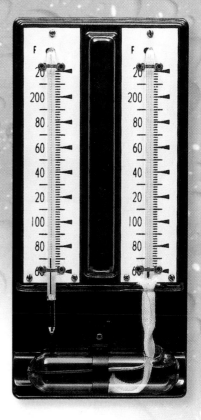

Aneroid Barometer

This instrument is more sensitive to changes in air pressure than Torricelli's mercury barometer. The word aneroid means "non-liquid." This barometer is made of a metal box from which most of the air has been removed. Changes in air pressure outside the box cause it to expand or contract, moving a needle on a dial. The numbers on the dial show what height a column of mercury would be at that air pressure. ▼

Thermometer

Thermometers can measure air temperature because matter expands when heated. Most thermometers are closed glass tubes containing liquids such as alcohol. The liquid expands and rises when it is heated by the air around it. Numbers on a Fahrenheit or Celsius scale next to the tube tell you the temperature in degrees. ▶

▲ *Weather data is transmitted by radio waves to a monitor, where it can be read easily.*

During the 1900s, great advances were made in developing equipment for observing and reporting the weather. Also, mathematicians and scientists developed mathematical equations that used weather data to forecast the weather. Once solved, the equations would provide predicted data—a forecast. The complex calculations took too much time to be practical until computers were developed in the 1940s. Meteorologists now use computers to quickly solve mathematical equations and make weather forecasts.

Today, weather data collection is highly computerized and automated. Electronic measuring devices and monitors, such as the one to the above left, have largely replaced traditional instruments. For example, a thermal sensor is often used in place of a thermometer. Tiny wires in the sensor expand in response to the temperature. Data from the sensors can be fed automatically into computers to make forecasts.

Upper Atmosphere Data

As early as the 1890s, meteorologists knew that weather near Earth's surface related to winds high in the atmosphere. In the 1930s, the Weather Bureau paid pilots bonuses to fly above 5,500 meters to observe high-altitude weather. Unfortunately, the pilots suffered from lack of oxygen at this altitude and many passed out. A safer way to gather high-altitude data was to launch balloons that carried instruments.

Today, around the world, hundreds of small instrument packages—each containing special sensors and a radio transmitter—are still lifted aloft twice daily. They measure temperature, wind direction, wind speed, and moisture as each balloon drifts into the upper air. The data is radioed to computers and transmitted around the world.

◄ *People at hundreds of weather stations around the world—including this one in Antarctica—release weather balloons at exactly the same time, twice a day. The data collected by weather balloons is extremely important in making forecasts.*

In an airport control tower, radar tracks flying airplanes. Radar uses radio waves, which bounce off objects like an echo. By measuring the time the signal takes to return, the distance to the object can be calculated. What flying objects are meteorologists looking for? They are looking for precipitation that can be found when radar bounces off rain or snow.

Doppler radar is an advanced type of radar that not only locates the presence of a storm but also tracks the direction the storm is moving. As shown below, precipitation moving toward the radar reflects radio waves at a higher frequency than does precipitation moving away from the radar. Doppler radar detects these differences. You can see on the Doppler radar screen below that these different frequencies appear as different colors. By watching the movement of precipitation and winds within a storm, meteorologists can better predict violent weather.

What difference can you see in the reflected radio waves from these two clouds? ▼

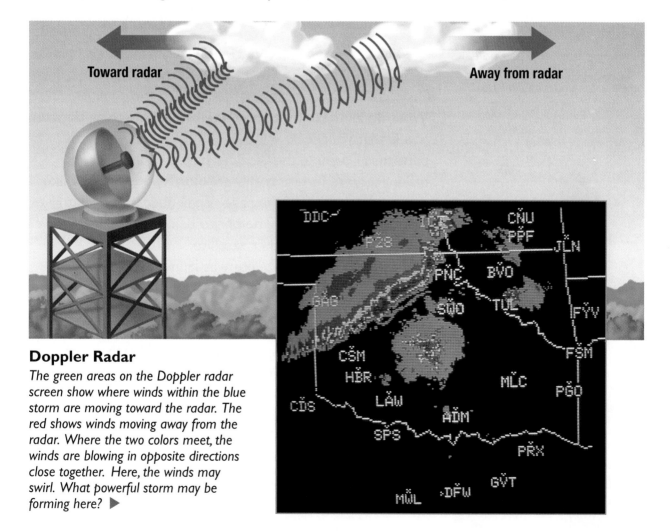

Toward radar

Away from radar

Doppler Radar

The green areas on the Doppler radar screen show where winds within the blue storm are moving toward the radar. The red shows winds moving away from the radar. Where the two colors meet, the winds are blowing in opposite directions close together. Here, the winds may swirl. What powerful storm may be forming here? ▶

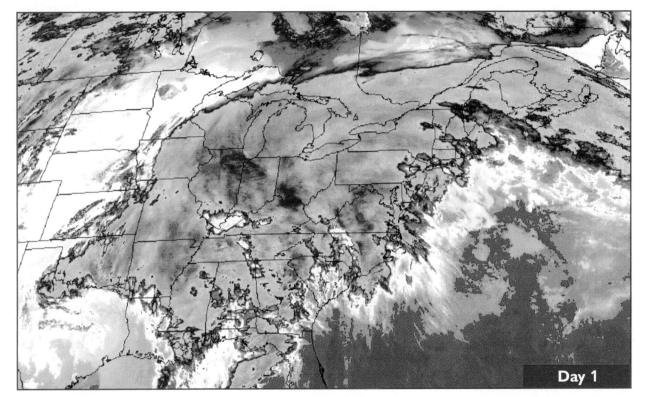

Day 1

▲ *The satellite views on these two pages have been color-enhanced. Red represents the most precipitation and blue represents the least. These images were taken one day apart.*

Winds blow around the globe. Warm, moist air near the equator rises and moves toward the poles. Cold, dry air from the polar regions drifts toward the equator. What do all these movements tell you? One thing they tell you is that your local weather is influenced by weather patterns all around the world. Therefore, in order to make accurate forecasts, meteorologists need a view like the one at the top of the page. They need a tool that gives them the "big picture." The photo below to the left shows one such tool—a weather satellite.

The first weather satellite was launched in 1960. It carried television cameras and stored the pictures on tape for later broadcast on Earth. Since then, many weather satellites have been launched. Some orbit Earth quickly, sending data about an entire path around Earth every 110 minutes. Other satellites, called geostationary

Weather Satellites

◄ *Weather satellites not only detect large weather systems across the globe but also monitor worldwide vegetation and determine damage to the environment. Almost anyone with a computer can access satellite information.*

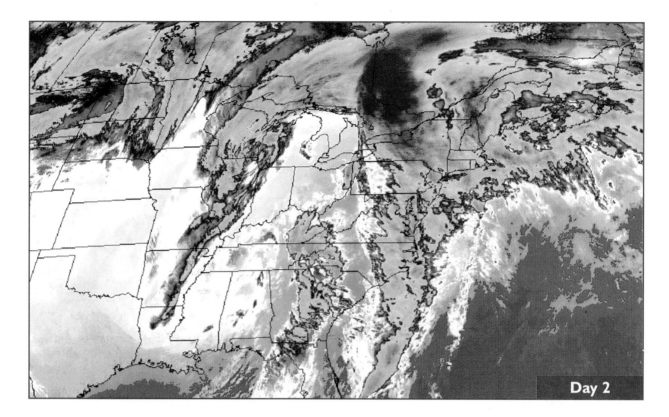

Day 2

satellites, are fixed over certain areas of the earth. They move at the same speed as Earth rotates. Therefore, these satellites send data only about the areas over which they are fixed.

Today, a network of satellites uses radio signals to beam images back to weather stations on Earth. They show movements of water vapor or provide a color analysis of the world's ocean temperatures. Compare the satellite photos on these two pages. They were taken one day apart. What kind of movement do they show? What are some advantages to using satellite images such as these?

Lesson 3 Review

1. How have forecasting techniques changed over time?
2. What tools are currently used to collect weather data?
3. How do scientists collect data about the upper atmosphere?
4. **Context Clues**
   Write a definition of *geostationary satellite*. Tell what context clues you used to figure out the definition.

Measuring Relative Humidity

Process Skills

- estimating and measuring
- observing
- collecting and interpreting data
- inferring

Materials

- safety goggles
- cheesecloth
- 2 thermometers
- 2 rubber bands
- milk carton with hole
- water

Getting Ready

In this activity, you will make a psychrometer, an instrument that is used to determine relative humidity. Review the information about humidity on pages C12 and C13 before you begin this activity.

Follow This Procedure

1 Make a chart like the one shown. Use your chart to record your observations.

Wet bulb (°C)	Dry bulb (°C)	Difference (°C)	Relative humidity (%)

2 Put on your safety goggles. Tie a piece of cheesecloth around the bulb end of a thermometer. The thermometer will have two "tails" of cheesecloth hanging from it. Position these tails at the back of the thermometer. This is your wet-bulb thermometer (Photo A).

Self-Monitoring

Does the cheesecloth tightly cover the bulb of the thermometer?

3 Slide two rubber bands onto the milk carton.

4 Locate the side of the milk carton with a hole cut into it. Slip the wet-bulb thermometer under the rubber bands, just above the hole. Push the cheesecloth "tails" of the wet-bulb thermometer through the hole in the carton (Photo B).

5 Slip another thermometer under the rubber bands on the milk carton as shown in Photo B. This is your dry-bulb thermometer. You will use it to **measure** air temperature.

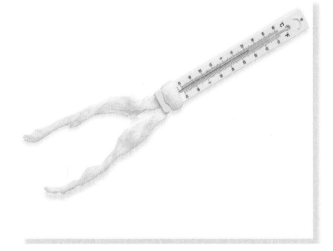

Photo A

⑥ Add water to the milk carton to a point just below the hole in its side. Make certain the cheesecloth tails from the thermometer extend into the water. Set the milk carton in a place where it will not be disturbed.

⑦ After a few minutes, the cheesecloth around the thermometer bulb will feel wet. **Observe** the change in the temperature of the wet bulb as water evaporates from the cheesecloth.

⑧ When the temperature reading of the wet-bulb thermometer stops changing, **collect data** from the two thermometers by recording the temperature readings in your chart. Then calculate the difference between the two temperature readings and record it in your chart.

⑨ Use the Relative Humidity table to determine relative humidity. Record the relative humidity in your chart.

Interpret Your Results

1. Explain why the wet-bulb thermometer reading is lower than the dry-bulb thermometer reading.

2. Make an **inference.** If the difference between the wet-bulb reading and the dry bulb reading is large, is the air relatively dry or relatively humid?

Photo B

Relative Humidity (percent)

Dry bulb (°C)	Difference between wet and dry bulb readings (°C)									
	1	2	3	4	5	6	7	8	9	10
18	91	82	73	65	57	49	41	34	27	20
19	91	82	74	65	58	50	43	36	29	22
20	91	83	74	67	59	53	46	39	32	26
21	91	83	75	67	60	53	46	39	32	26
22	92	83	76	68	61	54	47	40	34	28
23	92	84	76	69	62	55	48	42	36	30
24	92	84	77	69	62	56	49	43	37	31
25	92	84	77	70	63	57	50	44	39	33

Inquire Further

What would the difference be between wet-bulb and dry-bulb thermometer readings if the relative humidity were 100 percent? Develop a plan to answer this or other questions you may have.

Self-Assessment

- I followed the directions to make a psychrometer for measuring relative humidity.
- I **observed** the change in the wet-bulb thermometer.
- I **measured** and recorded the temperatures of the two thermometers.
- I used my **data** and the table to determine the relative humidity.
- I **inferred** the relationship between relative humidity and a large change in the wet-bulb temperature reading.

What's the Big Idea?

You will learn:

- how fronts and pressure systems affect weather.
- how technology is used to forecast weather.
- how to use weather maps to forecast weather.

Weather typically moves from west to east across the United States. ▼

How Are Weather Forecasts Made?

OH NO! It was supposed to be sunny today! You know only too well that weather forecasts aren't correct all of the time. Even with today's technology, forecasters can't know every weather condition that affects a prediction—but forecasts are getting better!

Fronts and Pressure Systems

Sometimes you may have been outside on a warm day and felt the temperature drop many degrees in a matter of minutes. What happened? The warm air didn't change—it moved out! Cooler air moved in.

At this moment, the air that surrounds your school and home is part of an air mass. An **air mass** is a very large body of air that has similar properties or weather conditions throughout. Air masses are huge—two or three of them can cover an entire country. Meteorologists track the movement of air masses to help predict the temperature, humidity, and air pressure of the area into which they are moving.

Los Angeles

Phoenix

Cold Air Mass

Cold Front

Warm Air Mass

Warm Front

When a warm air mass meets a cold air mass, the air in the different masses usually doesn't mix. The reason is because the properties of the two air masses are different. A boundary, or **front**, forms between the two different air masses. The dramatic drop in temperature described at the beginning of this lesson resulted as a cold front moved across the area. A cold front forms where a cold air mass moves into a warm air mass. A warm front forms where a warm air mass moves into a cold air mass.

How do fronts and air masses explain the weather you see at different places in the picture? Let's start with Los Angeles. Yesterday, a cold front passed through, causing thunderstorms. Today, Los Angeles is enjoying clear skies and cooler temperatures. Now the cold front is passing through Phoenix. The denser, cooler air wedges itself under the warmer air and lifts it. If the warm air is moist enough, cumulonimbus clouds may form and produce thunderstorms. That's what is happening in Phoenix. The storms may be violent but last less than an hour. About 400 kilometers to the east, a warm front has just passed through Dallas. The warm air mass glides up over the cold air mass. The rise is gradual and extends for many kilometers. Stratus clouds and precipitation extend almost all the way to New Orleans.

Weather generally moves across the United States from west to east. This movement is caused by the wind patterns across the earth. Use what you know about weather to predict the weather tomorrow for all the places in the picture.

Glossary

front (frunt), the boundary between warm and cold air masses

Glossary

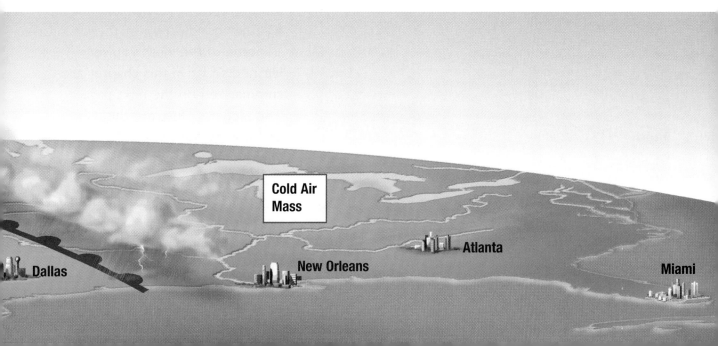

Dallas

Cold Air Mass

New Orleans

Atlanta

Miami

Air masses and fronts are major clues that you, as well as meteorologists, can use to forecast the weather. A third major clue has to do with air pressure systems. Certain weather is associated with lows and highs. For example, as winds blow into a low, warm air is rising. This upward flow of air often creates clouds and precipitation. On the other hand, a high usually brings fair weather. The heavier air of a high pushes downward and is usually colder and drier.

Technology and Weather Forecasts

To predict the weather, a forecaster relies on technology available through the National Weather Service (NWS). The picture below represents some of the newest technology from the NWS. The group of sensors is one of about 900 Automated Surface Observing Systems (ASOS) installed at airports nationwide to gather, process, and distribute weather data. ASOS equipment gathers information on cloud cover, visibility, temperature, humidity, air pressure, wind speed and direction, and precipitation.

ASOS data are recorded automatically each minute and reported directly to NWS offices. At the offices, the data are fed into the Advanced Weather Interactive Processing System (AWIPS). What's so special about AWIPS? This system allows forecasters to have access to and efficiently use all the weather data collected around the world to predict local weather conditions.

Some of the ideas you've learned so far in this chapter are summarized on the next page. The pictures illustrate the role technology plays in gathering weather data, processing it, analyzing it to make forecasts, and sharing all this information with others.

Automated Surface Observing Systems consist of sensors that transmit weather data directly to the National Weather Service. ▼

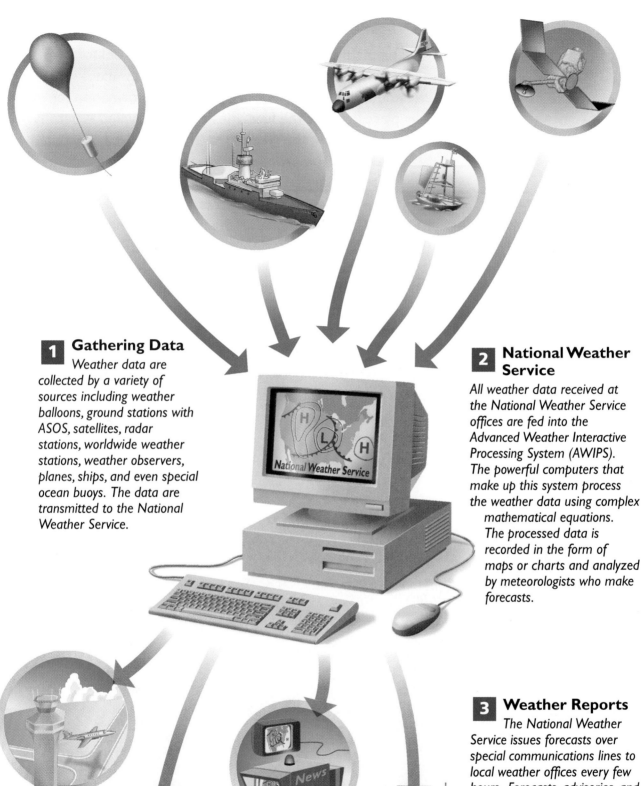

1 Gathering Data

Weather data are collected by a variety of sources including weather balloons, ground stations with ASOS, satellites, radar stations, worldwide weather stations, weather observers, planes, ships, and even special ocean buoys. The data are transmitted to the National Weather Service.

2 National Weather Service

All weather data received at the National Weather Service offices are fed into the Advanced Weather Interactive Processing System (AWIPS). The powerful computers that make up this system process the weather data using complex mathematical equations. The processed data is recorded in the form of maps or charts and analyzed by meteorologists who make forecasts.

3 Weather Reports

The National Weather Service issues forecasts over special communications lines to local weather offices every few hours. Forecasts, advisories, and warnings are then transmitted to airports, radio stations, television stations, newspapers, military bases, and other nations.

National Weather Service

Using Weather Maps

The picture on pages C28–29 is a useful tool for understanding what fronts are and how they affect weather. However, it doesn't give much information for any places except the few cities on the drawing. A better way to represent the weather over a large area is with a weather map. You probably have seen many kinds of weather maps in newspapers and on TV. Different maps may use slightly different symbols, but they likely all use symbols similar to those on the map on the next page. What weather information is included on this map? Use the key to find out.

Notice on the map that fronts extend from lows. Find a cold front and a warm front. What kind of weather is occurring along the fronts? Is this what you would expect? The map also shows a stationary front. Such a front occurs when an air mass stops moving. Precipitation may occur for several days along a stationary front. Where do you think the weather shown in the photo below is occurring?

This storm is most likely occurring along a cold front or in a low-pressure area. ▼

Weather Map

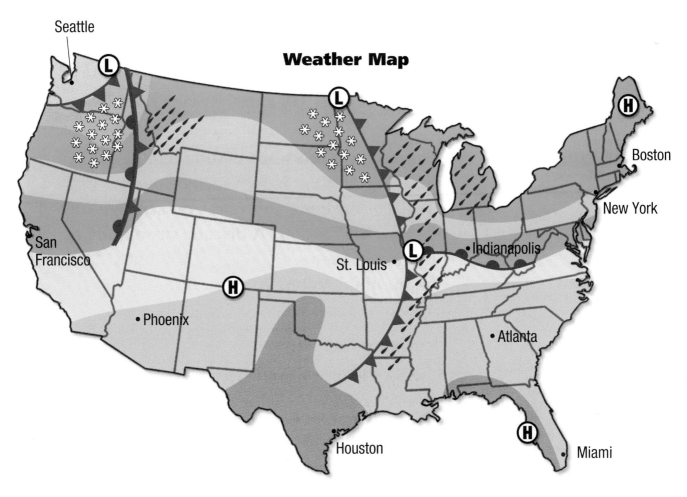

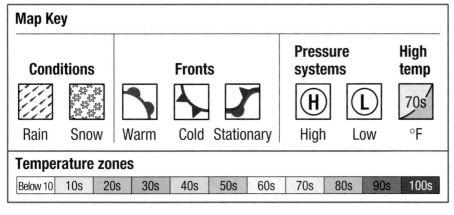

Map Key

Conditions		Fronts			Pressure systems		High temp
Rain	Snow	Warm	Cold	Stationary	High	Low	°F

Temperature zones

| Below 10 | 10s | 20s | 30s | 40s | 50s | 60s | 70s | 80s | 90s | 100s |

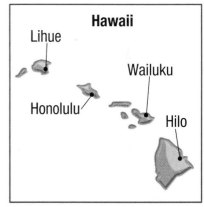

Hawaii

Lihue
Wailuku
Honolulu
Hilo

Lesson 4 Review

1. How do fronts and pressure systems affect weather?

2. How is technology used to forecast weather?

3. How can you use weather maps to forecast weather?

4. **Percent**
   What percentage of the states in the map above have temperatures in the 90s?

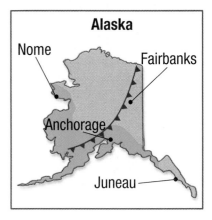

Alaska

Nome
Fairbanks
Anchorage
Juneau

You will learn:

- how different types of storms develop.
- how to be safe in severe weather.

Lesson 5

What Happens During Severe Weather?

Huge cumulonimbus clouds had been building all day. Now they are overhead. The sky darkens and takes on strange hues of gray and green. A distant siren adds to the eerie scene. **virrrRRR** What's happening? What will you do?

Types of Storms

As you learned in the last lesson, storms often accompany fronts and low-pressure systems. Thunderstorms, for example, form either along a cold front or within a warm air mass, as warm, moist air rises quickly. The rapid, continuous condensation of water vapor produces tall cumulus clouds, like the one in the picture to the left. The tops of the clouds may be more than 15,000 meters high. Here, the clouds are made of ice crystals, while the lower portions of the clouds are made of water droplets. The ice crystals and water droplets grow as they collide with other crystals and droplets. Eventually, they become large enough and heavy enough to fall. The ice melts when it falls through warmer air in the lower portion of the cloud. The melted ice joins the other drops as rain.

The falling rain pulls cold air with it, producing downward air currents called downdrafts. Meanwhile, warm air continues to rise, producing updrafts. If you've ever been in an airplane flying through a storm cloud, these rising and falling air currents likely produced a bumpy ride.

Updrafts and downdrafts are responsible for another characteristic of thunderstorms—lightning. The moving air causes electrical charges to build in the cloud. Notice in the picture how negative and positive charges are distributed throughout the cloud. When the difference

Lightning results when positive and negative electrical charges flow between a cloud and the ground, between different clouds, or within the same cloud. ▼

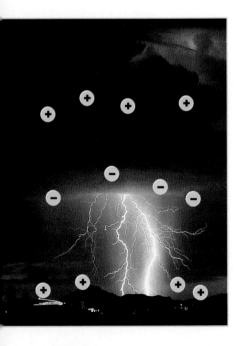

between the negative and positive charges is great enough, electrons flow between them. This momentary flow of electrons is an electric current called lightning. The streak of lightning heats the air along its path tremendously, causing the air to expand explosively. This expansion of air produces a sound wave you hear as thunder.

Storms can contain layers of air that move at different speeds. When this happens, air between the layers can start rolling like a pencil across a table. It is believed that a tornado forms when a strong updraft lifts one end of the rolling air. A **tornado** is a violent, funnel-shaped cloud with extremely strong winds.

A tornado might last only a few minutes, but the destruction it causes can be devastating. Although the tornado itself moves an average of only about 60 kilometers per hour, the swirling winds within the tornado can reach 500 kilometers per hour. These winds can lift a roof off a building. Flying debris breaks windows, which allows the wind inside. The wind can push out on the walls and push up on the roof. Only the foundation may be left.

Meteorologists have much to learn about tornadoes. Researchers, such as T. Theodore Fujita, shown here, are working to predict when and where these storms will occur. Some progress has been made. As you learned in Lesson 3, Doppler radar is a helpful tool for seeing where tornadoes are likely to form.

▲ The dark appearance of a funnel cloud is caused by the density of cloud particles and by soil and debris being swept up by the winds.

▲ T. Theodore Fujita uses dry ice and fans to generate model tornadoes. These models provide clues about how real tornadoes form.

Glossary

Glossary

hurricane (hėr′ə kān), a large tropical storm that forms over warm oceans and whose winds have a velocity of at least 110 kilometers per hour

Tornadoes are the most destructive storms, but hurricanes are the most powerful. A **hurricane** is a large tropical storm that forms over warm oceans and whose winds reach at least 110 kilometers per hour. Hurricanes are more powerful than tornadoes because of their huge size—usually at least 200 kilometers across.

Like other severe storms, hurricanes form around very low-pressure areas. The warm, moist ocean air spirals upward around the low and forms the cloud pattern you see in the satellite picture below. These circulating clouds bring high winds and heavy rain. The strong, steady winds over the ocean produce large waves that add to the destruction along the coast, as you can see below.

When the hurricane moves over land, it is no longer fed by warm, moist ocean air. The condensation of water vapor that gave the hurricane much of its energy stops occurring. After a couple of days, the storm loses power and the spiraling pattern of winds breaks up.

Much of a hurricane's damage is caused by huge waves that sweep over the shoreline, bulldozing everything in its way. ▶

◀ *In this photo, you can see that few clouds form in the center, or eye, of a hurricane. The eye is an area of relative calm while the storm rages all around.*

Safety in Severe Weather

Storms may be interesting to watch, but they are dangerous. Safety precautions should be taken seriously. The greatest danger of thunderstorms comes from lightning. So get indoors away from open windows and doors whenever a thunderstorm approaches. Avoid touching telephones, appliances, or metal plumbing—lightning can travel easily through these objects. If you're outside and unable to get indoors, do not seek shelter under a tree. Lightning tends to strike the highest objects in an area. If you're in the open, you may be the highest object. So lie down on the ground or crouch in a low area, such as a ditch. If you are swimming or in a boat, leave the water immediately—water conducts electricity.

Meteorologists keep a careful watch on developing weather conditions. If conditions are favorable for a tornado to form, the National Weather Service issues a tornado watch. A watch means you should be alert to rapid weather changes and plan for your safety. When a tornado has been sighted, the NWS issues a tornado warning. This is a time to take action. Read the safety tips to the right to find out what you should do.

Unlike tornadoes, people usually have several days to prepare for a hurricane. The NWS tracks a hurricane to predict where it will hit land. Mobile homes, vehicles, or boats are not safe places to be during a hurricane. Get into a sturdy building that can withstand strong winds and high, crashing waves. If you live in a low-lying area, you may need to leave your home until after the storm.

 Tornado Safety Tips

- **Seek shelter indoors in a basement or an interior room, such as a bathroom or closet, at the lowest level.**

- **Stay away from windows and get under anything that can protect you from flying objects.**

- **Avoid wide-span roofs when in public buildings.**

- **Abandon vehicles and mobile homes.**

- **Huddle in a ditch, under an overpass, or near something solid if there is no shelter nearby.**

Lesson 5 Review

1. How do thunderstorms, tornadoes, and hurricanes develop?

2. List two safety precautions each for a thunderstorm, a tornado, and a hurricane.

3. **Cause and Effect**
   Moving air in updrafts and down drafts causes electrical charges to build up in clouds. What effect does this buildup of charge cause?

Chapter 1 Review

Chapter Main Ideas

Lesson 1
• Extreme weather can create hazards and affect leisure and work activities.
• People can plan for their safety when weather extremes are predicted.

Lesson 2
• Wind is air moving from a region of high pressure to a region of low pressure.
• Warmer air can hold more humidity than cooler air.
• Most precipitation begins as snow. The temperature of air through which the precipitation falls determines the type.

Lesson 3
• Simple observations of nature evolved into forecasting, with the help of instruments such as the barometer.
• Currently, sophisticated computers and electronic measuring devices are used along with traditional weather tools.
• Data about the upper atmosphere is collected by balloon-carried weather instruments, by Doppler radar, and by weather satellites.

Lesson 4
• Fronts move from west to east, carrying weather changes.
• Weather data is widely collected and transmitted to the National Weather Service (NWS). There computers analyze the information to predict weather.
• The weather information shown as symbols on weather maps can be used to determine fronts and pressure systems.

Lesson 5
• When warm, moist air rises quickly along cold fronts, thunderstorms and tornadoes develop on land and hurricanes develop over the ocean.
• When severe weather threatens, seek appropriate shelter and heed advice from the National Weather Service.

Reviewing Science Words and Concepts

Write the letter of the word or phrase that best completes each sentence.

a. air mass	h. front
b. air pressure	i. humidity
c. anemometer	j. hurricane
d. barometer	k. meteorologist
e. dew point	l. psychrometer
f. Doppler radar	m. relative humidity
g. forecast	n. tornado

1. An instrument that measures wind speed is the ___.
2. An instrument for determining relative humidity is the ___.
3. A(n) ___ measures air pressure.
4. A person who studies the weather is called a(n) ___.
5. The boundary between warm and cold air masses is a(n) ___.
6. A large body of air having similar properties is a(n) ___.
7. A type of radio transmission that tracks precipitation is called ___.

8. The temperature at which a volume of air cannot hold any more water vapor is called the ___.

9. A(n) ___ is a tropical storm with high winds that forms over oceans.

10. A measurement that compares the amount of water vapor in air with the amount it can hold at a given temperature is called ___.

11. The amount of water vapor in the air is ___.

12. A prediction of what the weather will be like in the near future is a(n) ___.

13. As air cools, the ___ increases.

14. A violent, funnel-shaped cloud is a(n) ___.

Explaining Science

Write a paragraph or an outline that explains these questions.

1. How do forecasts help people?

2. What conditions affect weather?

3. How has weather technology evolved?

4. How do meteorologists forecast weather?

5. What characteristics and precautions are associated with thunderstorms, tornadoes, and hurricanes?

Using Skills

1. **Observe** local weather for one week. Determine the **percentage** of rainy days.

2. **Communicate.** Write a list of questions for an interview with a meteorologist about the history of forecasting.

3. **Collect data** on the latest weather developments in nearby cities to the west of where you live by listening to weather reports or interpreting a weather map. Then **predict** what kind of weather you can expect soon.

Critical Thinking

1. **Evaluate** the role of the telegraph in weather forecasting. Write a paragraph explaining whether or not the telegraph was an important development.

2. Imagine a hurricane has just been predicted for your area. **Make a decision** about what safety precautions you should take. List the precautions.

3. Imagine you are a meteorologist. Draw a flow chart showing the **sequence** of steps involved in making a forecast.

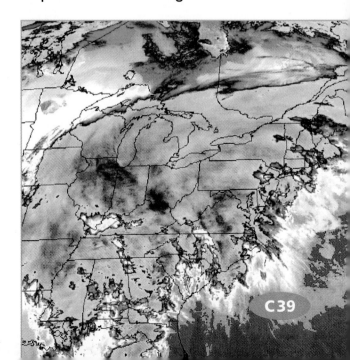

Shifting Sands

It's easy to see how these layers of sand are made. But what about the layers of sand, rocks, and other minerals in Earth's crust? How were those made? Which were laid down first?

Chapter 2
Earth Processes

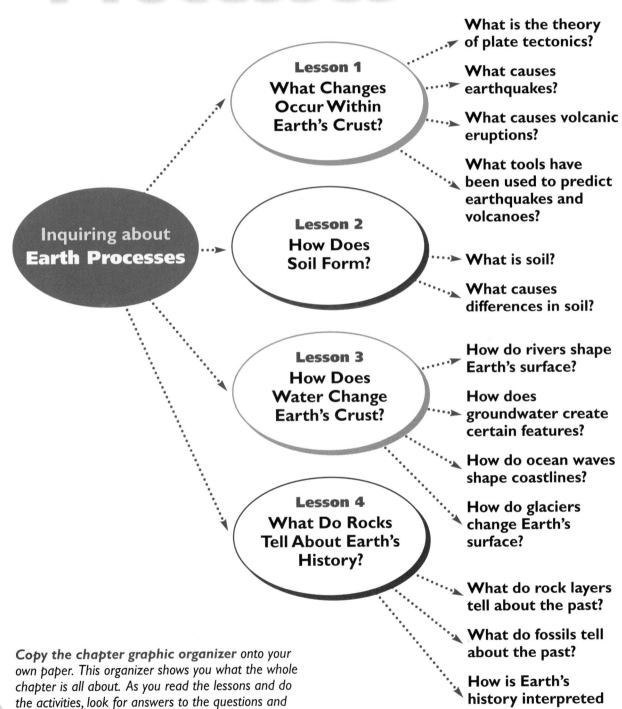

Inquiring about Earth Processes

Lesson 1
What Changes Occur Within Earth's Crust?

What is the theory of plate tectonics?

What causes earthquakes?

What causes volcanic eruptions?

What tools have been used to predict earthquakes and volcanoes?

Lesson 2
How Does Soil Form?

What is soil?

What causes differences in soil?

Lesson 3
How Does Water Change Earth's Crust?

How do rivers shape Earth's surface?

How does groundwater create certain features?

How do ocean waves shape coastlines?

How do glaciers change Earth's surface?

Lesson 4
What Do Rocks Tell About Earth's History?

What do rock layers tell about the past?

What do fossils tell about the past?

How is Earth's history interpreted and recorded?

Copy the chapter graphic organizer onto your own paper. This organizer shows you what the whole chapter is all about. As you read the lessons and do the activities, look for answers to the questions and write them on your organizer.

Exploring Properties of the Earth's Mantle

Process Skills

- estimating and measuring
- observing

Materials

- newspaper
- masking tape
- water
- plastic graduated cup
- spoon
- cornstarch
- wax paper

Explore

① Cover your desk or lab table with several sheets of newspaper. Tape the newspaper in place.

② **Measure** 25 mL of water into a plastic graduated cup.

③ Add 3 heaping spoonfuls of cornstarch to the water. Mix well with the spoon until no powder is visible, as shown in the photo.

④ Place a piece of wax paper on top of the newspaper on your desk. Place one spoonful of the substance in the cup on the wax paper. **Observe** what happens to the substance.

⑤ Pick up the substance, and roll it into a ball in your hands. Observe what happens as you touch it and as it sets in your hand.

Reflect

1. What characteristics did you find as you observed the substance?

2. Did the substance act like a liquid or a solid? Explain.

? Inquire Further

What would happen if you made a large ball of the substance? How could you make the ball keep its shape? Develop a plan to answer these or other questions you may have.

Using Graphic Sources

When reading science, it is important to know how to use graphic sources. A graphic source can be a picture, a diagram, or a chart that provides an example or explains an idea. As you read Lesson 1, *What Changes Occur Within Earth's Crust?*, be alert for key words such as *shows, look at, illustrates,* and *notice.* These words give you a purpose for using the graphics.

Example

Look at the picture below from page C45. Read the title and caption. Look for labels or callouts. Then pay attention to details in the graphic. Finally, ask yourself what main idea can be learned from studying the graphic.

Earth's Tectonic Plates

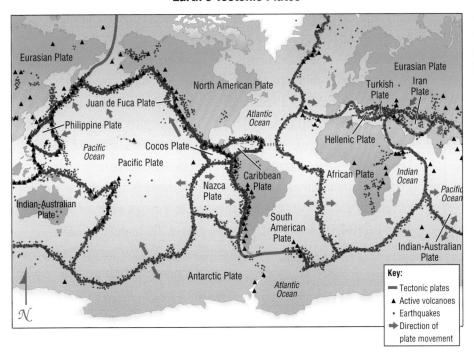

◀ *Earth's plates can move toward, away from, or past each other, as the arrows indicate.*

Talk About It!

1. How can graphics help you understand what you are reading?

2. What did you learn about plate movement from looking at the graphic?

You will learn:

- **what the theory of plate tectonics is.**
- **what causes earthquakes.**
- **what causes volcanic eruptions.**
- **what tools have been used to predict earthquakes and volcanoes.**

Glossary

lithosphere (lith′ə sfir), the solid rocky outer layer of the earth that includes the crust

plate tectonics (plāt tek ton′iks), theory that states that the lithosphere is broken into plates that move

Lesson 1

What Changes Occur Within Earth's Crust?

Mmmm . . . Bite into a warm piece of French bread. **CRUNCH!** That's the crust—the thin outer layer of bread. Now think about a different kind of crust—not quite so tasty!

Plate Tectonics

Earth's crust is the outermost solid layer of the planet. It includes the features shown on the globe below—the continents and the floor of the oceans. Scientists think that 200 million years ago, Earth's crust was much different from what the globe below shows. Seas existed where mountains now stand, and the land consisted of one large mass instead of separate continents. Obviously, Earth's crust has changed a lot in the past 200 million years. What explains these changes? The answer begins with the crust.

The crust is actually the upper part of a thicker solid layer called the **lithosphere**. The lithosphere is not a continuous layer. Rather, it is broken into about 20 sections called plates. Each plate is a huge slab of rock that includes the crust. These plates fit together like pieces of a jigsaw puzzle, as you can see on the map at the top of the next page. However, unlike jigsaw puzzles, the plates don't stay put. The solid plates float on a layer of partly melted rock. This idea that the lithosphere is broken into moving plates is called the theory of **plate tectonics**. This theory explains much about how the earth looks.

This globe shows Earth as it appears today. Scientists have gathered evidence suggesting that Earth did not always look like this. ▶

C44

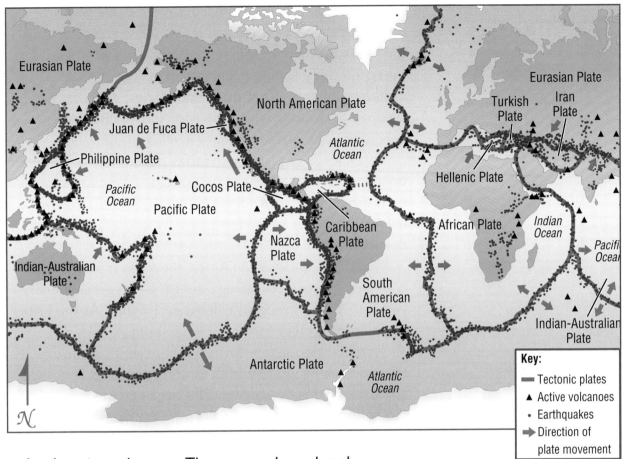

Key:
- ▬ Tectonic plates
- ▲ Active volcanoes
- • Earthquakes
- ➡ Direction of plate movement

Look again at the map. The arrows show that the plates move in different directions. Scientists have determined that some plates move at an average rate of about 2 centimeters per year. That's only about as fast as your fingernails grow! Others move as fast as 15 centimeters per year. You can see why it takes millions of years for continents to change positions very much.

What makes the plates move? The picture below shows one explanation—slow-moving convection currents beneath the plates. A convection current is a movement of matter. In a convection current, hot matter rises, while cooler matter sinks. The differences in temperature cause material to move in a circular pattern. This process occurs in the mantle when hot, partially melted rock rises up to the plates and spreads out sideways. The spreading carries the plates along. As the magma spreads, it cools. Then the material sinks back into the mantle, where it heats and rises again.

Earth's Tectonic Plates

▲ Earth's plates can move toward, away from, or past each other, as the arrows indicate.

Convection Currents

Convection currents in the mantle cause hot, partially melted rock to move, dragging continents and ocean floors with it. ▼

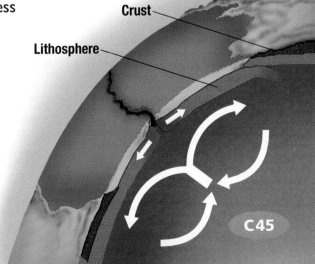

Crust

Lithosphere

C45

Glossary

fault (fôlt), a crack in the earth's crust along which rock moves

Tremendous changes in Earth's crust occur at plate boundaries where two plates meet. Here, the plates may slide past each other, collide, or move away from each other. All this grinding, pushing, and pulling of rock produces many faults at plate boundaries. A **fault** is a break in rock along which the rock moves. By this definition, each plate boundary itself is a huge fault.

Three kinds of plate boundaries occur. A fault boundary is an area where two plates are moving past each other. The San Andreas Fault in California, shown below left, is one of the few places where a fault boundary occurs on land.

The Great Rift Valley in Africa, shown in the circle below is an example of a spreading boundary—an area where two plates are moving away from each other. As the plates move apart, a valley forms between them.

A colliding boundary forms where two plates move toward each other. Often, ocean crust collides with the crust that forms continents. The ocean crust sinks below the continental crust and melts into the mantle. The continental crust buckles into mountains. If two continental plates collide, they both buckle into tall mountains, such as the Himalayas shown below.

At the San Andreas Fault in California, two plates move past each other at a relatively fast rate of 5 centimeters per year. What events often occur near this boundary? ▼

◀ New crust is created at spreading boundaries such as the Great Rift Valley in Africa. As spreading continues, the valley will widen and deepen and form a sea.

At colliding boundaries, plates push against each other and fold rock layers into huge mountains. That's how the Himalayas formed. They continue to grow taller as the Eurasian Plate and Indian-Australian Plate continue to collide. ▶

Earthquakes

You don't have to worry about a crustal plate zooming by—plates move very slowly. In fact, sometimes they don't move at all for many years. Parts of the plates may snag on each other. Then pressure builds until the rock breaks and lurches forward several centimeters all at once. This sudden movement makes the crust shake. The sudden shaking or vibrating of the earth's crust is an earthquake. Most earthquakes occur near plate boundaries, as you can see on the map on page C45. This outcome makes sense because earthquakes occur as rock moves suddenly along faults, and most faults are at plate boundaries.

How does an earthquake cause the kind of damage you see in the building below? When a huge slab of rock suddenly slips, the energy that has been building up is quickly released. The drawing shows how the released energy travels in waves away from the point where the rock first moves—the **focus**. The waves make the ground shake, just as waves in water make a small boat bob up and down.

Glossary

focus (fō′kəs), the point along a fault where rock first breaks or moves, causing an earthquake

▲ When an earthquake occurs, waves of energy move outward from the focus in all directions.

During an earthquake, waves can cause the ground to roll, shake, or suddenly lift. These movements can destroy roads and other structures, such as this building. ▶

Glossary

seismograph
(sīz′mə graf), instrument that records the strengths of the earth's movements, based on the amount of energy released

Richter scale
(rik′tər skāl), a scale used to compare the strengths of earthquakes

Zigzag lines on this seismograph provide a record of waves produced by an earthquake. ▼

During an earthquake, as the energy waves move away from the focus, they lose energy. If you stood directly above the focus of a strong earthquake, you'd be the first person to feel the ground shake. A person standing many miles away from you wouldn't feel the earthquake as quickly or as strongly.

About 800,000 earthquakes occur around the world every year. Most of them are too weak to be felt by people. However, an instrument called a **seismograph** can measure and record even the slightest vibration from the weakest earthquake. A seismograph includes a revolving paper drum like the one shown in the picture on the left. When the ground shakes, a pen records these movements as a pattern of zigzag lines.

When you hear about an earthquake that occurred, the description usually includes a number on the Richter scale. The **Richter scale,** shown below, is a series of numbers used to describe the strength of an earthquake. The number is based on the total amount of energy released. The scale was developed in the 1930s by an American scientist named Charles Richter. Each whole number on the scale represents an earthquake ten times stronger than an earthquake with a number below it. For example, an earthquake that measures 6.0 on the Richter scale is ten times stronger than one that measures 5.0. The strength of the earthquake at any particular place depends on how close that place is to the focus of the earthquake—the closer to the focus, the stronger the waves and the more damage they can do.

Richter Scale

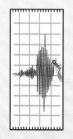      

Richter Number	2.0–2.9	3.0–3.9	4.0–4.9	5.0–5.9	6.0–6.9	7.0–7.9	8.0–8.9
Damage caused by earthquake near focus	Not felt but recorded	Felt by few people	Felt by most people	Slight damage	Much damage	Great damage	Buildings destroyed

Volcanoes

A volcano is an opening on the surface of the earth through which magma rises. As the map on page C45 shows, volcanoes are closely related to plate movement. Like earthquakes, most of the world's volcanoes practically outline the plate boundaries, both on the continents and on the ocean floor.

What's the connection between volcanoes and plate tectonics? At colliding boundaries, one plate often sinks beneath the other plate. The sinking crust melts into magma as it enters the mantle. Since hot magma is less dense than solid rock, the magma rises through openings in the crust. Gases within the magma cause pressure to build, much the way pressure builds when you shake a can of carbonated beverage. Eventually the pressure is so great that magma breaks through the surface as lava, exploding like the drink spraying from an opened can.

Volcanic eruptions on land, such as Mt. Arenal in Costa Rica, shown below, are big news items. However, you never hear about most volcanic activity because it takes place at spreading boundaries on the ocean floor. These eruptions are gentle compared to those at colliding boundaries. Lava quietly flows out onto the surface of the plate, adding new crust to the ocean floor. The hot lava cools when it reaches the cold ocean water and hardens into rock.

A volcano can build as ash and lava gather around the opening. However, some eruptions are so explosive, they destroy part of the volcano. ▼

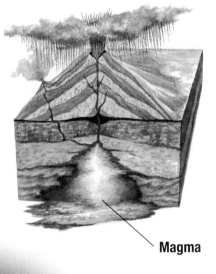

Magma

The Ruins of Pompeii

One of the most destructive volcanic eruptions in history took place in Italy in the year A.D. 79, when Mount Vesuvius suddenly exploded. The towns of Pompeii and nearby Herculaneum were quickly buried beneath ash and mud. Plaster casts made of some of the victims provide an eerie reminder of Earth's awesome power. ▼

Predicting Earthquakes and Volcanoes

History of Science

Earthquakes and volcanic eruptions have plagued civilizations throughout recorded history. People have long recognized that lives could be saved if these destructive events could be predicted. Today, scientists have many complex instruments to monitor earthquakes and volcanoes. Some instruments that are more than a thousand years old, however, seem just as ingenious.

First Seismograph

In the year A.D. 132, a Chinese inventor named Chang Heng presented this earthquake detector to the Chinese court. When the ground shook even slightly, the dragon on the side closest to the focus would drop a ball into the open mouth of a toad below. From this action, people were able to identify the direction from which the earthquake came. A series of pins, levers, and pendulums inside the vase made this seismograph work. ▶

Tiltmeter

Another device to help scientists predict volcanic eruptions is a tiltmeter. It detects changes in the slope of a volcano. A change in the slope of a volcano might mean that magma is moving within the mountain. ▶

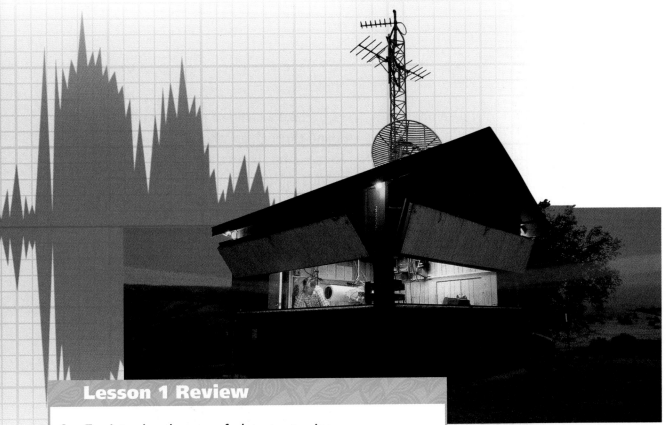

Lesson 1 Review

1. Explain the theory of plate tectonics.

2. What causes earthquakes?

3. What causes volcanic eruptions?

4. What are some tools that have been used to predict earthquakes and volcanoes?

5. **Graphic Sources**
   Find the map on page C45. On which plate is the United States? In which direction is that plate moving?

Laser Detector

▲ Today, lasers are used to detect earth movement. A beam of laser light is aimed at a reflector on the other side of a plate boundary. Scientists record the time it takes for the light to travel this distance and back. Any change might mean that an earthquake is coming. Lasers are also used to detect bulges in a volcano—a sign that an eruption may occur soon.

Making a Model Seismograph

Process Skills

- making and using models
- predicting
- observing
- inferring

Materials

- safety goggles
- shoe box
- cafeteria tray
- masking tape
- ruler
- rubber bands
- 2 washers
- clay
- felt tip pen

Getting Ready

In this activity, you will make a model seismograph.

Review the information about seismographs on page C48.

Follow This Procedure

1 Make several copies of the chart shown below. These will become seismograms that record the intensity of your "earthquakes."

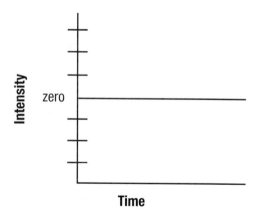

2 Put on your safety goggles. Make a **model** of a seismograph. Stand a shoe box on a cafeteria tray. Tape the shoe box to the tray.

3 Tape a ruler to the top of the shoe box.

4 Make a chain of rubber bands. Place one band through another. Thread the end of one rubber band through itself. Pull both bands tight to form a knot. Add 4 more rubber bands (Photo A). Add a washer to each end of the chain.

5 Wrap a small strip of clay around the top of a pen. Attach each washer to the strip of clay by pressing it into the clay. Hang the chain over the ruler.

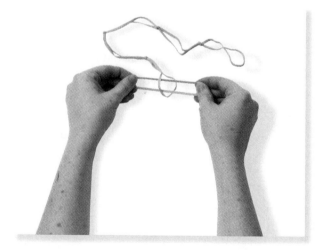

Photo A

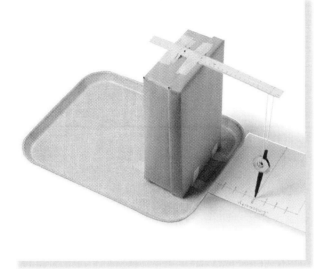

Photo B

⑥ Place your chart under the pen (Photo B). Adjust the clay and the washers so that the tip of the pen will just touch the paper. Tape the chain in place on the ruler. Remove the cap from the pen.

⑦ Allow each partner to practice pulling the sheet of paper across the table at an even speed. **Predict** what will happen if the tray is moved while someone pulls the paper.

⑧ Make a seismogram of a simulated earthquake. Have one student pull the paper. Have a partner gently shake the tray to produce an "earthquake." **Observe** how the seismograph and seismogram are affected by each earthquake.

⑨ Take turns producing earthquakes and recording their intensities on different seismograms. Compare the different seismograms you make.

Interpret Your Results

1. What did you observe as your seismograph recorded an earthquake? What do the lines on your chart represent?

2. Describe how you and your partners were able to produce different seismograms.

3. Make an **inference**. Tell how seismographs are used to measure the energy released during an earthquake.

⟨?⟩ Inquire Further

How could you use your seismograph to tell how many seconds or minutes an earthquake lasted? Develop a plan to answer this or other questions you may have.

Self-Assessment

- I followed the directions to make a **model** seismograph.
- I **predicted** what would happen if the table moved while a partner pulled the paper under the pen.
- I **observed** the effects of simulated earthquakes on the seismogram.
- I compared the seismograms of different earthquakes.
- I made an **inference** about how a seismograph can be used to indicate the energy released during an earthquake.

What's the Big Idea?

You will learn:
• what soil is.
• what causes differences in soil.

Lesson 2

How Does Soil Form?

Mix together tiny bits of weathered rocks and dust. Add some dried leaves and decayed animal parts. Sprinkle in some animal droppings and fragments of animal fur or bird feathers. Mix well. **YUK!** What IS this? It's a "recipe" for soil.

Soil

In Lesson 1, you learned about changes in Earth's crust that happen when processes occur deep within the Earth. Soil formation is a process too, but it occurs on Earth's surface. Soil forms when rocks, animal life, plant life, air, water, and chemicals interact. Like many earth processes, soil formation takes a long time. The interactions that formed the handful of soil in the picture occurred over thousands of years.

What do you see in this handful of soil? Look closely. Try to find some of the "ingredients" mentioned above. Perhaps all you see is something that gets your hands dirty. Actually, soil is as important to life as water, air, and sunlight. Most life on Earth depends on soil. Without soil, animals—and you—would have few plants to use for food or shelter. Think about it! What have you used today that depended on soil in one way or another? Did you think about the paper of this book?

Soil is a mixture of weathered rock and decayed plant and animal matter that formed over a long period of time. The diagram on the next page will help you understand why soil takes thousands of years to form.

Soil is a mixture of grains of rock and organic matter. How many different ingredients can you find in this handful of soil? ▼

Soil Formation

1. *Soil formation begins with the break up of rock.*

2. *At the surface, rock weathers into stones and grains of sand. This material mixes with moss and other organic matter to form a thin layer of soil. More plants take root in the developing soil, which attracts more animal life. Their decaying bodies and wastes make the soil thicker and richer.*

3. *As weathering continues and organic matter builds, the soil becomes fully developed and can support a greater variety of plants.*

As you see in the first picture, soil begins as rock. When rock is exposed at or near the surface, it begins to break apart. Water and gases in the air form a weak acid that eats away at rock. Also, water in the cracks of rock expands as it freezes and wedges the rock apart. This group of processes that break down rock is called **weathering.** The processes of weathering gradually break rock into smaller and smaller fragments. Mosses and a few other types of vegetation grow on these fragments. The rock weathers further into grains of sand, silt, and clay.

In the next stages, the soil becomes thicker and richer. As moss and other plants die, they decay and become part of the soil. Insects, worms, bacteria, and fungi start to live among the plant roots and rock particles. Seeds of grasses and shrubs blow into the area, take root, and grow. As organisms die, their decaying bodies form dark-colored organic matter called humus. Animal droppings add to the growing richness of the soil, which can now support a greater variety of plant life. As worms and insects burrow, they mix the humus with the fragments of weathered rock to form the rich fertile soil you see in the last drawing.

Glossary

weathering
(weᴛʜ′ər ing), group of processes that break rocks into smaller pieces

Glossary

Differences in Soil

Have you ever seen different layers of soil where a hill was cut to form a road? Perhaps you noticed plants growing in a dark layer at the top. The layers below may have been lighter in color. These layers of soil make up a soil profile. Most soil profiles show three distinct layers.

Usually, the dark top layer, called topsoil, is rich in humus. When rain water filters through the topsoil, it often carries dissolved minerals down to the second layer. The third and lowest layer is partly weathered rock that is just beginning the long, slow process of changing into soil from the rock below.

Notice the different thicknesses and types of soil layers in the soil profiles shown below. The differences depend on the climate and type of rock from which the soil formed. Other factors that affect a soil profile include the shape of the land, the amount of humus available, and how long the soil has been forming.

Soil Profiles
Compare these two profiles. ▶

Topsoil

Subsoil

Bedrock

Lesson 2 Review

1. What is soil?

2. What causes differences in soil?

3. **Graphic Sources**
   According to the picture on page C55, how does soil formation affect plant life at the surface of the soil?

How Does Water Change Earth's Crust?

Paddle in ... paddle out ... paddle in ... paddle out ... What a **FANTASTIC** day to be on the water! Be careful, though, the current is **STRONG.** Watch out for that boulder! A stream flows into the river up ahead. The waters will be choppy there.

Rivers

A river is always coming from one place and going someplace else. The river shown here begins as a trickle of melting snow high on a mountain many kilometers upstream. Gravity causes the water to flow downhill. Along the way, more rainwater and melting snow running off the land join it. The trickle grows into a stream. Smaller streams that started the same way join the main stream, bringing it more water and making it grow. The stream grows this way to become the river you see here. How do you think the river below will look 30 kilometers downstream?

Streams that join larger streams are called tributaries. The main river and all its tributaries make a river system. The satellite photo to the right shows that a river system looks like the branching of a tree. The river system ends where the main river flows into the ocean or a lake.

You will learn:
• how rivers shape Earth's surface.
• how groundwater creates certain features.
• how ocean waves shape coastlines.
• how glaciers change Earth's surface.

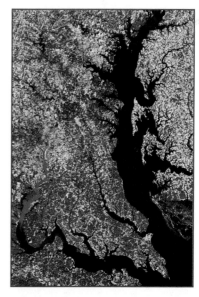

▲ The people in the canoe below are on a mid-size tributary. Where might they be located on this satellite view of the river system?

Glossary

drainage basin
(drā′nij bā sin), the land area from which a river system gets its water

sediment (sed′ə mənt), rock and soil carried by water

The land area from which a river system gets its water is called a **drainage basin.** A drainage basin is like a sink. All water that falls into the sink eventually flows down toward the drain. Similarly, most water that flows over the land of a drainage basin eventually flows into the main river. The Mississippi River has the largest drainage basin in the United States. Its basin covers nearly two-thirds of the country!

If you were watering a garden with a hose, would you turn the hose on full blast? Most likely, you wouldn't because you know that the force of the water would dig up the soil and uproot the plants. Running water is a powerful sculptor. The running water of rivers wears away—or erodes—rock and soil. These materials, which are called **sediments,** flow with the river and make it an even better sculptor of the land. The pictures on these two pages show how a river changes the landscape along its route.

V-Shaped Valleys

The beginning, or headwaters, of a river is often in a mountainous or hilly area. The water flows fast because the slope is steep. The fast-moving water has much power to erode and cuts steep V-shaped valleys. The sediment is carried downstream. What other features are common in this part of the river? ▶

Floodplains

◀ Further downstream, the slope of the river is gentler. The river is wider because by now many tributaries have joined it. The river forms looping bends called meanders, which erode the sides of the valley and make it wider. During floods, the stream overflows. A low-lying area called a floodplain forms.

Meanders and Oxbows

◀ The river moves much more slowly as it flows over flatter land toward the sea. Flooding is more common, and the floodwaters erode a wide floodplain. The river erodes mostly at its sides, causing well-developed meanders. Horseshoe-shaped oxbow lakes form when the river takes a straighter course, cutting off a meander.

Glossary

groundwater
(ground wȯ tər), water in the ground near Earth's surface

aquifer (ak′wə fər), a layer of rock in which ground water can accumulate and flow freely

water table
(wȯ′tər tā′bəl), the top of an aquifer

Ground Water

Not all of the water from rain and snow flows over the land into rivers. Some of the precipitation slowly sinks into the ground through the soil. It keeps seeping down through tiny cracks and spaces in the rock until it finally reaches a layer of rock that it can't pass through. This rock prevents the water from traveling down any farther. Now the water is part of an underground system of water called **groundwater**.

Notice in the drawing below how groundwater gathers in spaces in the rock layer above the impermeable rock. A layer of rock where groundwater can accumulate and flow freely is called an **aquifer**. You can see that groundwater accumulates to a certain level in an aquifer. The top of this water level is the **water table**.

The shape of the water table generally follows the shape of the land. It rises under hills and sinks under valleys. At times, the water table is visible at the surface. Groundwater near the surface may form swamps, marshes, and other wetlands, or it can flow out as a spring on hillsides.

Groundwater fills the air spaces in soil and in rock, like water in a sponge. ▼

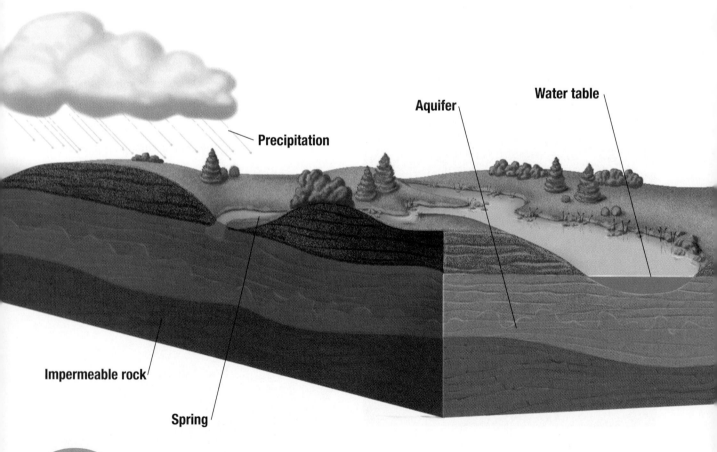

Precipitation

Aquifer

Water table

Impermeable rock

Spring

Half of the population of the United States depends on groundwater for its drinking water. People get this water by drilling wells into the aquifer. Groundwater flows into the well and is pumped to the surface. As you can see in the diagram, the bottom of a well must be placed below the water table. When too much water is used, or during dry seasons, the water table drops. Then the well goes dry until rain adds more water to the aquifer. Then the water table rises.

Groundwater produces some unusual features. The picture to the right shows one of them. If groundwater lies close to hot volcanic rock or magma, the water gets heated. The heated water rises to the surface and erupts in a fountain of hot water and steam called a geyser. The 200 geysers in Yellowstone National Park are a sign of this area's magma beneath its surface.

You know that water on Earth's surface erodes surface rock. Groundwater erodes rock too. When rainwater seeps downward through limestone, it dissolves calcium and other minerals in the limestone. Over time, groundwater carves out huge caverns. How huge? One cavern in Carlsbad Caverns, New Mexico, can hold the Unites States Capitol Building!

▲ *Old Faithful in Yellowstone National Park, Wyoming, is a geyser that erupts regularly when groundwater seeps into spaces near hot rock. Geysers are also found in Iceland and New Zealand.*

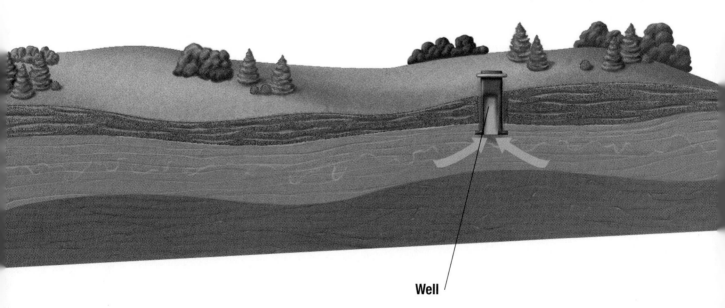

Well

Ocean Waves

Rivers and some groundwater eventually flow to the ocean. The water that empties into the ocean brings sediments and a mixture of dissolved elements with it. Some of these dissolved elements combine to form new substances. Sea animals and plants use a dissolved element, calcium, to carry on their life processes, such as building shells or forming bones. Other elements form minerals on the ocean floor that are important resources for humans.

The waves shown here tell you something else about ocean water—it is powerful and in constant motion. Energy is needed to produce any kind of wave. If you hold the end of a rope and shake it, your arm provides the energy that makes the wave on the rope. Wind provides the energy that causes most ocean waves. The longer and stronger the wind blows, the larger the waves.

Ocean waves may travel thousands of kilometers before finally breaking on shore. ▼

A water particle moves up and down in a circle as a wave passes. Near shore, the circle flattens because of friction with the sea floor. ▼

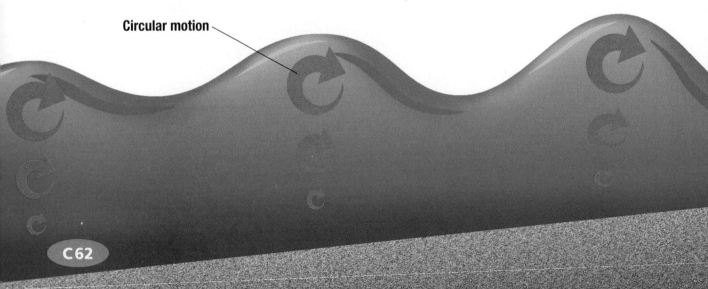

Circular motion

C62

Waves rolling toward the ocean shore may look as if they are moving forward. Actually, water is moving up and down in a wave. Remember the rope? As you shake the rope to make a wave, the wave moves forward, but the rope does not. The same thing happens in water waves. The diagram shows that water particles remain in about the same place, turning in a circle as the energy in each wave pushes forward.

Notice that waves get taller as they approach the shoreline. That's because the water is getting shallower. Friction with the ocean bottom slows the bottom of the wave. The top of the wave moves slightly ahead and tumbles forward, breaking on shore. These waves are breakers. Water in a breaker no longer moves in circles; it actually moves forward onto the shore.

Waves constantly breaking against the shore created the rocky formations you see in the picture above. Waves also carry stones and sand that grind away at the rocky coast. While waves wear away the land in some places, they build it up in other places. For example, waves that strike the shore at an angle help move sand along the shoreline, forming sandy beaches.

▲ Wave erosion formed the steep, jagged cliffs you see here. How will these features change as erosion continues?

Breaker

Glossary

glacier (glā′shər), a large mass of moving ice

moraine (mə rān′), a ridge formed when a glacier deposits its sediments

Glaciers

You've seen how Earth's crust is changed by rivers, groundwater, and ocean waves. Water as a flowing mass of ice can also change the crust.

In some cold areas, the amount of snow that falls each year is greater than the amount that melts. Over hundreds or thousands of years, the accumulating snow packs into ice. A large mass of slowly moving ice, called a **glacier**, forms. The picture below shows Mendenhall Glacier, which formed high in the mountains of Alaska. Gravity causes this river of ice to move slowly—several centimeters a day—downhill. A glacier also moves when pressure created by the heavy ice causes the bottom of the glacier to melt. The glacier then glides across the melted ice.

Glaciers shape the land in many ways. As glaciers move, they scrape away loose fragments of stone and soil. The loose materials are carried by the glacier. When the glacier melts, it deposits, or drops, its load of sediments in ridges along the sides and end of the glacier. This type of glacial deposit is called a **moraine**.

The Mendenhall Glacier near Juneau, Alaska, moves slowly down the mountain, carving and reshaping the valley as it goes. The dark stripes are rocks that have broken off the sides of the valley. The number of stripes tells you how many smaller glaciers have joined this one. ▼

◄ The rounded, U-shape of this valley in Canada is a sign that a valley glacier once existed here. The glacier gouged out a valley that is deeper, wider, and rounder than the one that existed before.

▲ Jagged rocks trapped in the bottom of a glacier scraped grooves into this bedrock as a glacier slowly moved over it. The grooves indicate the direction the glacier was moving.

Other changes in Earth's surface happen as melted water beneath the glacier seeps into cracks of rock and freezes. As the freezing water expands, chunks of rock break loose and become frozen into the bottom and sides of the glacier. The rocks, which have been plucked and frozen onto the glacier, scrape across the bedrock to form the scratches and grooves you see here to the right.

As glaciers gouge out the earth during their lifetime, they reshape narrow V-shaped river valleys into rounded, U-shaped valleys like the one shown above.

Lesson 3 Review

1. How do rivers change Earth's surface?
2. How does groundwater create certain features?
3. How do ocean waves shape coastlines?
4. How do glaciers change Earth's surface?
5. **Graphic Sources**
   Why do the arrows in the waves on the bottom of pages C62–C63 flatten as they move toward shore?

Making a Model Glacier

Process Skills

Process Skills

- making and using models
- predicting
- observing
- inferring
- communicating

Materials

- small milk carton opened at the top
- water
- metric ruler
- pebbles
- modeling clay
- safety goggles
- rectangular pan
- sand
- gravel
- plastic spoon

Getting Ready

In this activity, you will model how glaciers erode land.

Follow This Procedure

1 Make a chart like the one shown. Use your chart to record your observations.

Glacier on clay		
Action of glacier	Prediction	Observations
Moving		

Glacier on rocky mountain		
Action of glacier	Prediction	Observations
Moving		
Melting		
After melting		

2 Pour water into a small milk carton to a depth of about 5 cm. Add a single layer of pebbles to the water in the carton. Freeze this water-and-pebble mixture to make a **model** glacier.

3 Press some modeling clay on a flat surface. Carefully remove your glacier from the milk carton and place it pebble-side-down on the clay (Photo A).

4 **Predict** what will happen if you move the glacier along the surface of the clay. Record and then test your prediction. Record your **observations.**

Photo A

5 Put on your safety goggles. Make a "mountain" in a pan from moistened sand and gravel.

6 Use a plastic spoon to make a narrow groove down the side of the mountain. This groove represents a valley carved by a stream. Place your glacier in the valley at the top of the mountain (Photo B). Slide the glacier down the valley. Observe and record what happens.

7 Replace your glacier in the valley at the top of the mountain. Softly press the glacier into the mountain top so it stays in place. Predict what will happen as the glacier melts. Record and then test your prediction. Be sure to record what happens to the surface of the mountain as well as to the sediment deposited.

8 Leave your setup where it will not be disturbed. Check it again after all the ice has melted. Note the location of the pebbles that were once part of the glacier. Record your observations.

Photo B

Interpret Your Results

1. In step 4, what happened to the surface of the clay?

2. Make an **inference**. Based on your observations, describe how a glacier may transport rocks and soil from one place to another.

3. Communicate. Discuss how your observations in this activity compare to features made by real glaciers.

Inquire Further

How would a sudden change in average temperature—either an increase or a decrease—affect the erosion due to a glacier? Develop a plan to answer this or other questions you may have.

Self-Assessment

- I followed the directions to make **models** of two types of glaciers.
- I **predicted** the effects of glaciers on two types of landscapes.
- I recorded my **observations.**
- I made an **inference** about glaciers and the transport of materials from one place to another.
- I **communicated** my ideas about how the activity results compare with land features made by actual glaciers.

You will learn:

- how rock layers tell about the past.
- what fossils tell about the past.
- how Earth's history is interpreted and recorded.

Lesson 4

What Do Rocks Tell About Earth's History?

Want to read a good story? It's quite a mystery. It has some of the **STRANGEST** characters you'll ever run across. The book is loaded with clues that could be **FUN** to figure out. You won't be able to carry the book in your backpack, though. The pages are **ROCKS!**

Rocks Tell About the Past

What's one of the first things you notice about the rock formation below? You probably noticed the different colored stripes. Each stripe represents a different layer of sediment that formed into sedimentary rock. What can you tell about these rock layers? For one thing, you can be fairly certain that the bottom layer of rock is the oldest.

The rock in these sedimentary layers was once at the bottom of an ancient sea. Forces probably due to plate movement raised the rock above sea level. Erosion then exposed the formation as it appears now. ▼

Shale

If a series of sedimentary layers are not overturned, the oldest layer is always at the bottom and the youngest layer is always on top. It's like putting T-shirts one at a time in a drawer—the shirt you put in first will be on the bottom of the pile, and it will have been there the longest.

To fully understand how rocks tell a story about past earth processes, it's important to know how rocks are made. Sedimentary rock forms over long periods of time as sediments are deposited and then pressed and cemented together. Each sedimentary layer provides a record of a past event.

For example, one kind of sedimentary rock—limestone—forms from pieces of seashells and dissolved shells, bones, and other materials that collect on the bottom of shallow oceans. So the layer of limestone you see on these pages was formed under an ancient ocean. The fine grains that make up another kind of sedimentary rock—shale—settle out of water far from shore, indicating that this rock formed in deeper waters. Likewise, sandstone, another sedimentary rock, tells of past deserts or shallow sandy shores.

Limestone

Sandstone

Fossils Tell About the Past

Forming Fossils

Some fossils form when dead organisms are covered with sediments, which harden into rock. The soft parts of the organism decay, leaving an impression in the rock. This impression can later be filled with other sediments that also harden, forming a fossil cast. As you can see below, the cast fossil resembles the actual organism. ▼

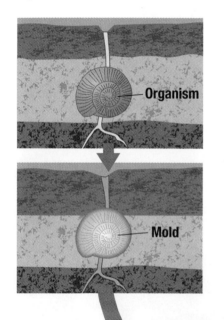

Organism

Mold

Cast

One of the most important stories that rocks tell is about the kind of life that existed when the rocks were being formed. How can such a story be told? Dead organisms often get buried by sediments that later become sedimentary rock. Traces of the organisms sometimes become preserved in the rock as fossils. Sometimes, a fossil is a shell, a bone, or part of a plant that was gradually replaced by rock. It can even be a track or trail, or petrified animal droppings. Usually, the soft parts of an organism decay or get eaten by other creatures quickly. As a result, they don't last long enough to become fossilized. Hard parts, such as shells, bones, teeth, and wood, have a better chance of becoming fossils. To the left, you can see one way fossils form.

Fossils help paleontologists learn about Earth's past environments. For example, fossils of shellfish found high in the Alps, Rockies, Andes, and Himalayas are evidence that the rock of these mountains formed under water. How can paleontologists tell whether an underwater environment was a river, lake, swamp, or open sea? By comparing fossils with similar organisms that exist today, scientists can make inferences about the specific environment in the past.

Fossils also provide a history of past climates. For example, rocks in Antarctica near the South Pole contain fossils of tropical plants. This evidence suggests that Antarctica must have been much warmer in the past than it is today. How do you think plate tectonics supports this conclusion?

Every rock formation can tell a story, but it may be only a chapter. Paleontologists are often more interested in the larger story—how the evidence at one place relates to evidence found at other places around the world.

Therefore, they compare fossils in layers of rock from different areas, as shown below. Index fossils are especially helpful for comparison. An **index fossil** is a fossil of an organism that existed on Earth for a relatively short time and in many places. Therefore, an index fossil can be used to establish the age of any rock in which it is found. Index fossils can be used to match rock layers that appear in different places.

Glossary

index fossil
(in′deks fos′əl), a fossil of an organism that existed on Earth for a short time over a large geographic area

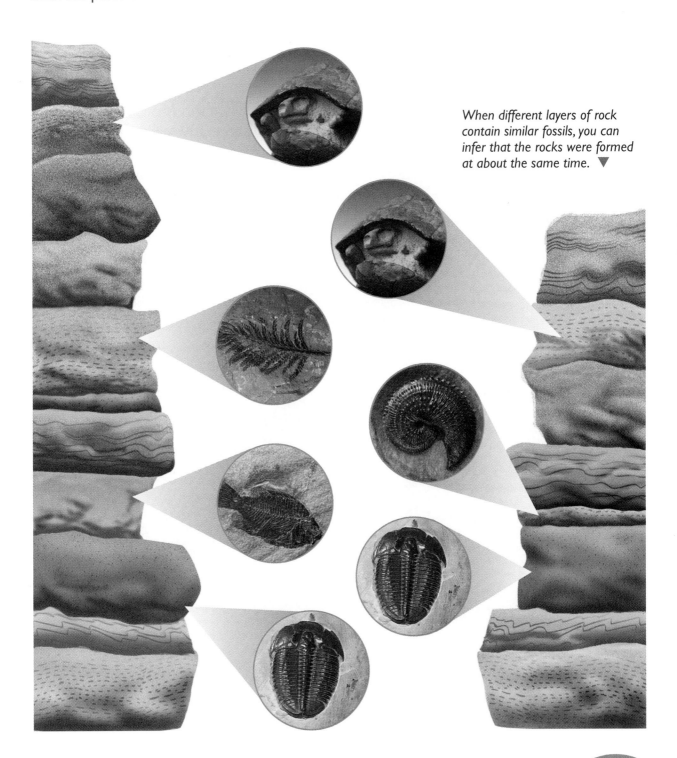

When different layers of rock contain similar fossils, you can infer that the rocks were formed at about the same time. ▼

Interpreting Earth's History

While scientists figure out the order in which certain rock layers were formed, they also explain the fossil evidence the rocks contain. Fossils help scientists reconstruct an accurate picture of ancient life forms and their environments. These reconstructions are based on knowledge of life forms that live today.

For example, compare the three images shown below. The fossil, on the bottom left, is of a creature called *Archaeopteryx*. The fossil clearly shows that *Archaeopteryx* had characteristics of both a dinosaur and a bird. The limestone that contained this fossil suggests the animal lived about 150 million years ago on the shore of a shallow pond in Germany. From this fossil, scientists and an artist reconstructed how the animal might have looked at the time of its death. Another drawing shows how this birdlike dinosaur might have looked and acted in life. Both drawings are based on our knowledge of birds, reptiles, and other animals today.

An interpretation of the fossil record indicates that birds probably evolved from dinosaurs. Archaeopteryx was a birdlike dinosaur that had wings and feathers like a bird's, but teeth and claws like a meat-eating dinosaur's. ▼

Artist rendering

Fossil

Artist reconstruction from fossil

Scientists also use fossils and the rocks that contain them to form theories about why certain life forms disappeared, or became extinct. For example, the trilobite fossil pictured to the right shows a hard-shelled sea creature that lived over 500 million years ago. Trilobites lived with other marine life when warm, shallow seas covered much of the earth's surface. The trilobites disappeared about 250 million years ago. Most paleontologists think they became extinct because shallow seas dried up when mountains were uplifted due to plate movement.

The trilobite, a multi-legged sea animal, became extinct about 250 million years ago, most likely because of mountain building that drained the seas. This fossil of the bottom surface of a trilobite shows much detail. ▼

Another interpretation of the rock and fossil records explains the extinction of the dinosaurs about 65 million years ago. Many scientists think that a huge asteroid or comet hit Earth and produced a giant cloud of dust that blocked the sun's light. Temperatures dropped, plants died, and many other forms of life, including the dinosaurs like the one below, either froze or starved to death. Among the evidence for this theory is that an unusual amount of the element iridium is found in rocks that are 65 million years old. Iridium is rare on Earth but it is much more common in the rock of asteroids and comets. Also, scientists think they have found the huge crater that such an impact would have made—in the Yucatan Peninsula and the Gulf of Mexico.

◄ *Dinosaurs like this Oreodontia, existed for 150 million years. They became extinct about 65 million years ago. Many scientists think they know why.*

Glossary

geologic time scale
(jē ə loj′ik tīm skāl), a record of Earth's history based on events interpreted from the rock record and fossil evidence

History of Science

Scientists who attempt to interpret the rock and fossil evidence to determine Earth's history have a long period of time to account for. Earth has been around for about 4.6 billion years! No written records exist to tell when mountains were born or when seas covered continents. To record a history of such events, scientists have constructed a **geologic time scale.** The divisions of time on this scale are based on important events, such as the rise of new life forms and the formation of mountain ranges.

Geologic Time Scale

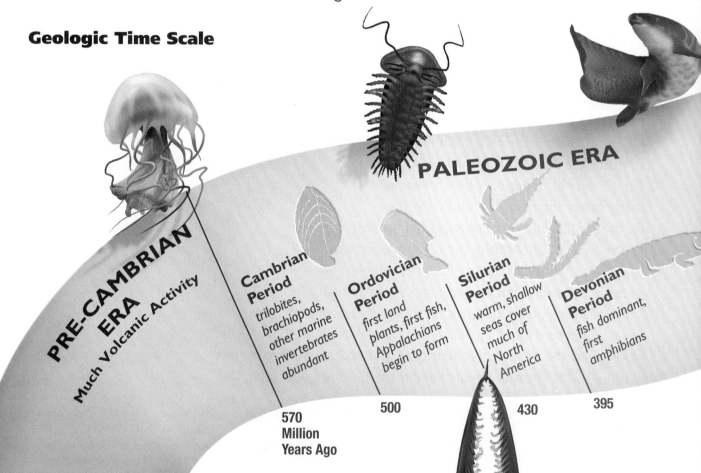

PALEOZOIC ERA

PRE-CAMBRIAN ERA
Much Volcanic Activity

Cambrian Period
trilobites, brachiopods, other marine invertebrates abundant

Ordovician Period
first land plants, first fish, Appalachians begin to form

Silurian Period
warm, shallow seas cover much of North America

Devonian Period
fish dominant, first amphibians

570 Million Years Ago

500

430

395

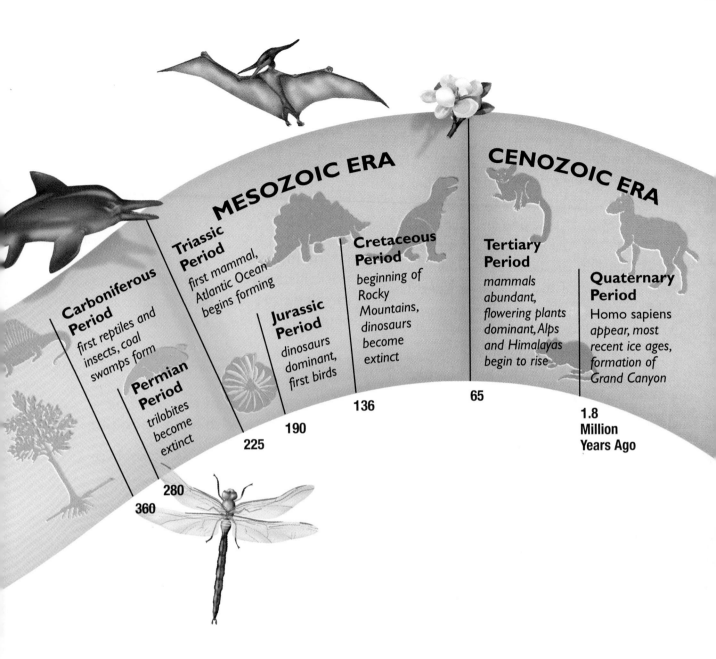

CARBONIFEROUS Period
first reptiles and insects, coal swamps form

Permian Period
trilobites become extinct

MESOZOIC ERA

Triassic Period
first mammal, Atlantic Ocean begins forming

Jurassic Period
dinosaurs dominant, first birds

Cretaceous Period
beginning of Rocky Mountains, dinosaurs become extinct

CENOZOIC ERA

Tertiary Period
mammals abundant, flowering plants dominant, Alps and Himalayas begin to rise

Quaternary Period
Homo sapiens appear, most recent ice ages, formation of Grand Canyon

360

280

225

190

136

65

1.8 Million Years Ago

Lesson 4 Review

1. What do rock layers tell about Earth's past?
2. What do fossils tell about Earth's past?
3. How is Earth's history interpreted and recorded?
4. **Graphic Sources**
   According to the geologic time scale above, when did dinosaurs become extinct?

Chapter 2 Review

Chapter Main Ideas

Lesson 1

• Earth's moving plates build up or tear down the earth's crust as they float toward, away, or past one another on partly melted rock in the upper mantle.
• Earthquakes are the release of energy that occurs as plates slip past one another while moving in opposite directions.
• Volcanoes are caused by molten rock that rises at plate boundaries.
• Seismographs and lasers are used to monitor earth movement.

Lesson 2

• Soil is a mixture of weathered rock and decayed organic matter that formed over a very long time.
• Soils differ due to the type of bedrock and climate present when they were formed, the amount of humus available, and the time the soil has been forming.

Lesson 3

• River systems drain large areas of land, eroding the soil and depositing material along the way.
• Groundwater erupts as geysers when it is heated by magma and forms underground caverns when it dissolves minerals in limestone.
• Wave action can erode rock or deposit sand to create certain features along coastlines.
• Glaciers erode land or deposit sediments.

Lesson 4

• When layers of rock remain untouched, the types of rock and their arrangement provide a history of how and when the rocks were formed.
• Fossils tell about life forms, climates, and environments of the past.
• Scientists make inferences about the earth's history and record it on a geologic time scale.

Reviewing Science Words and Concepts

Write the letter of the word or words that go with each definition.

a. aquifer
b. drainage basin
c. fault
d. focus
e. geologic time scale
f. glacier
g. groundwater
h. index fossil
i. lithosphere
j. moraine
k. plate tectonics
l. relative dating
m. Richter scale
n. sediment
o. seismograph
p. water table
q. weathering

1. Two forms of water than can erode the earth are ____ and ____.
2. The layer of rock that forms the earth's crust is the ____.
3. The theory of ____ explains how plates move over the mantle.
4. A crack in the earth's crust along which rock layers move is a(n) ____.
5. The ____ is a scale for measuring the strength of earthquakes.

6. The ___ is a record of earth's history.

7. A ridge formed from glacial deposits is a(n) ___.

8. The land area drained by a river system is a(n) ___.

9. The point along a fault where rock first breaks is the ___.

10. Permeable rock where groundwater accumulates and flows freely is a(n) ___.

11. The remains of an organism that lived for a short time over a wide area is a(n) ___.

12. Scientists use a(n) ___ to record the strengths of earth movements.

13. Determining the age of rock by comparing it with other rock layers is ___.

14. The process in which rocks are broken down is ___.

15. Rock and mineral carried by water are ___.

16. The top of an aquifer is the ___.

Explaining Science

Use drawings or write a paragraph that explains these questions.

1. How does the theory of plate tectonics explain changes in the earth's crust?

2. How does rock turn into soil?

3. What land features are created by water?

4. How do rocks provide a history of the earth?

Using Skills

1. Prepare a time scale on a wide strip of paper that shows your life history. **Use graphics** to show eras and periods such as "Growing Up Era" or "Middle School Period."

2. Write a letter to the editor **communicating** why methods should be taken to protect soil from erosion.

3. Use the **model** of convection currents shown on page C45 to explain why the earth's plates move.

Critical Thinking

1. Imagine horizontal layers of sedimentary rock with a vertical strip of a different kind of rock—igneous rock—running through the layers. **Apply** what you know about how rock is formed to **infer** the relative age of the igneous rock.

2. You discover rock layers at the top of a mountain containing fossils of shells and other marine life. **Draw conclusions** about the geologic history of the area.

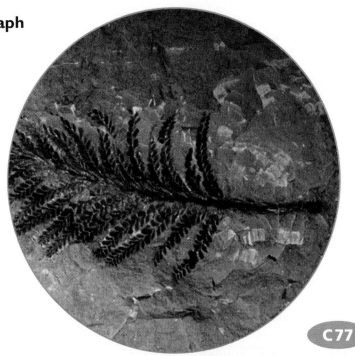

A Carnival Ride ?

What kind of ride is this boy on? Not an ordinary one! He's at the **NASA** Space Camp, learning about space travel. What can we learn from studying the universe? What do we already know?

Chapter 3
Exploring the Universe

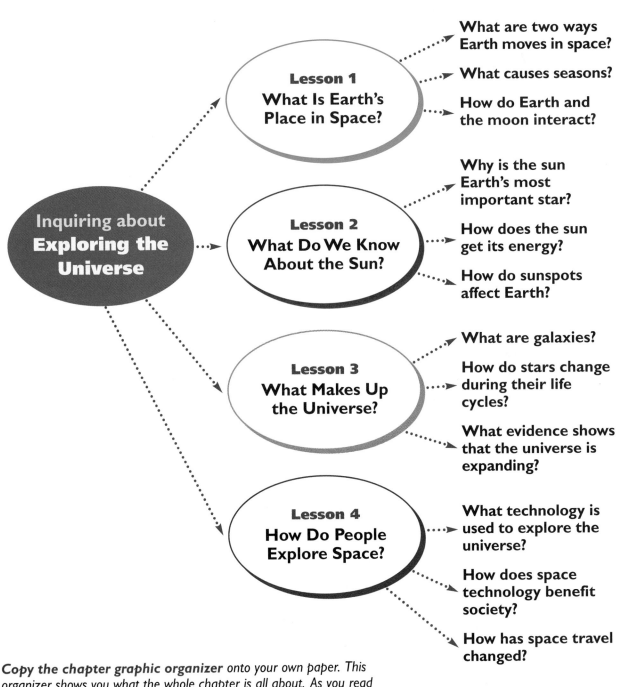

Inquiring about Exploring the Universe

Lesson 1
What Is Earth's Place in Space?

What are two ways Earth moves in space?

What causes seasons?

How do Earth and the moon interact?

Lesson 2
What Do We Know About the Sun?

Why is the sun Earth's most important star?

How does the sun get its energy?

How do sunspots affect Earth?

Lesson 3
What Makes Up the Universe?

What are galaxies?

How do stars change during their life cycles?

What evidence shows that the universe is expanding?

Lesson 4
How Do People Explore Space?

What technology is used to explore the universe?

How does space technology benefit society?

How has space travel changed?

Copy the chapter graphic organizer onto your own paper. This organizer shows you what the whole chapter is all about. As you read the lessons and do the activities, look for answers to the questions and write them on your organizer.

Exploring Lunar Eclipses

Process Skills

- making and using models
- observing

Process Skills

Materials

- compass
- cardboard
- marker
- scissors
- masking tape
- 2 plastic straws
- metric ruler
- flashlight

Explore

① Make a **model** of a lunar eclipse. Use a compass to draw two circles on a piece of cardboard. One circle should be about 3 cm in diameter. Label this circle *Moon*. The other circle should be about 8 cm in diameter. Use a marker to label this circle *Earth*. Cut out the circles to make two discs.

② Tape each cardboard disk to a straw.

③ Darken the room so that you can clearly see the lights and shadows in this demonstration.

④ One student should hold the Moon disk near the chalkboard or wall. A second student should stand about 1 m away and shine the flashlight directly at the Moon disk.

⑤ A third student should take the Earth disk and gradually move it across the beam of light illuminating the Moon. **Observe** the effect that the movement of the Earth disk has on the Moon disk.

Reflect

1. What part of the solar system does the flashlight represent in this activity?

2. What did you observe on the Moon disk when you passed the Earth disk between it and the light source?

? Inquire Further

Suppose you moved the Moon disk between the light and the Earth disk. What would you observe happening to the light on the Earth? Develop a plan to answer this or other questions you may have.

Large Numbers

Suppose you are the commander of a disabled spacecraft. Mission Control wants to know how far you are from Earth.

Your controls show that you are 45,000,000,000,000 km away. You report, "We are 45 trillion kilometers from Earth."

In order to use large numbers, you need to know the names of large **place values.** Look at the chart below. The digit 4 is in the ten-trillions place. It represents 4 ten-trillions, or 40,000,000,000,000. Where is the digit 5?

Math Vocabulary

place value, the multiple of ten telling how much a digit represents

Place Value

hundreds	tens	ones	hundreds	tens	ones	hundreds	tens	ones	hundreds	tens	ones	hundreds	tens	ones
	4	5	**0**	0	0	**0**	0	0	**0**	0	0	**0**	0	0
Trillions			**Billions**			**Millions**			**Thousands**			**Ones**		

Example

Find the place value of the *9* in Vega's diameter.

Diameters of Six Brightest Stars	
Name	**Diameter (mi)**
Sun	864,730
Sirius	1,556,500
Canopus	25,951,900
Alpha Centauri	1,037,700
Arcturus	19,888,800
Vega	2,594,200

Vega's diameter is 2,594,200 miles. The *9* is in the ten-thousands place. So, it represents 9 ten-thousands, or 90,000.

Talk About It!

1. Is there a name for every number, no matter how large? Explain.

You will learn:

- two ways Earth moves in space.
- what causes the seasons.
- how Earth and the moon interact.

Lesson 1

What Is Earth's Place in Space?

Hey! Stand still! What do you mean you can't do that? No matter how hard you try to stay in one place, Earth beneath you is moving. So, let's go for a spin! Spinning is just one way that Earth moves.

Earth's Motion

What do you know about the spheres shown below? You may already know that these spheres represent the nine planets that travel around the sun as part of our solar system. Perhaps you know that a band of small rocky objects called asteroids also moves around the sun. Of course, there's one place in the solar system you know quite a lot about—Earth! The third planet from the sun is the only planet scientists know of that supports life.

Notice the relative position of each planet from the sun. If this drawing were made to scale, the sun would be the size of a beach ball. Earth and Venus would be about the size of a marble, and Pluto would be only as large as a pin head. The distances between the planets would be different too. ▼

Earth and all objects in space are constantly rolling, tumbling, or moving in some way. All the planets spin, or rotate, on an imaginary line called an axis. As you can see on the next page, Earth's axis runs from the North Pole to the South Pole. Each planet rotates on its axis at a different speed. Earth takes 24 hours, or one day, to make one complete turn, or rotation.

Sun — Mercury — Venus — Earth — Mars — Jupiter — Saturn — Uranus — Neptune — Pluto

As Earth is viewed from above the North Pole, it rotates on its tilted axis in a west-to-east direction. In other words, Earth rotates from west to east. While Earth rotates, half of the planet faces toward the sun. This half of the planet experiences day. At the same time, the other half of the planet faces away from the sun, creating night. You can't feel Earth's spinning motion, but you can see signs of it. For example, Earth's rotation makes the sun appear to move across the sky from east to west. Most of the other planets also rotate in the same counter-clockwise direction, but they do so at different speeds and at different angles, or tilts.

Earth moves in another way too. The planets and asteroids travel, or revolve, around the sun in paths called orbits. Earth takes about 365 days, or one year, to complete its orbit around the sun. This trip is one revolution.

The speed of other planets in their orbits may be faster or slower than Earth's, depending upon the planet's distance from the sun. For example, take a look at Mercury, the sun's nearest planet. Mercury takes only 88 Earth days to revolve around the sun because it has such a small orbit. The most distant planet, Pluto, has the largest orbit. Pluto takes 90,700 Earth days to complete one revolution. So how many Earth years is a year on Pluto?

It certainly seems that everything in space is on the move! While Earth revolves around the sun, the moon revolves around Earth, and other moons revolve around their planets. In fact, the sun and the entire solar system are moving. So, sit back and enjoy the ride as you learn what all this motion means and where everything is going!

Axis

North Pole

South Pole

▲ Even though you can't really see the North and South Poles of Earth, it helps to imagine them. Picture Earth rotating around a pole, or axis, that is tilted.

Earth's Seasons

What do you notice in the picture below about the axis as Earth travels in its yearly orbit around the sun? Find a point where the North Pole leans toward the sun. At this point, the sun's rays strike areas north of the equator most directly, and the daylight hours are longer. The northern half of the world, or Northern Hemisphere, experiences summer. In the United States, you might be swimming, but in Argentina students will be putting on hats and gloves as they leave school. Why?

The seasons change as Earth tilts toward or away from the sun while making a revolution. A seasonal change occurs each time Earth moves one-fourth of the way around its yearly orbit. ▼

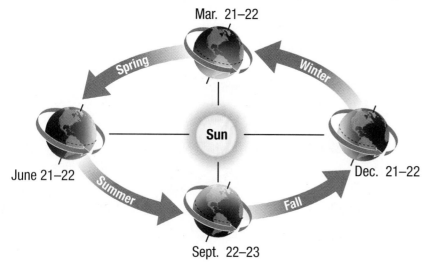

Mar. 21–22

Spring

Winter

June 21–22

Sun

Dec. 21–22

Summer

Fall

Sept. 22–23

Notice in the picture that when the Northern Hemisphere experiences summer, the southern half of the world, or Southern Hemisphere, is tipped away from the sun. The sun's light strikes that part of Earth at an angle that is much less direct, and the daylight hours are shorter. At this time, the southern half of the world has winter.

The seasons change as Earth's axis either leans toward or away from the sun—or leans somewhere in between—at different times throughout its orbit. People at the equator do not experience this change in seasons because the effect of the tilt of that area of Earth doesn't change as much.

Have you noticed that the amount of sunlight also changes as season's change? When it's summer in your part of the world, the sun is high in the sky. Daylight lasts longer than at other times of the year. During summer, you can enjoy playing ball or other activities outside longer. If you live in the Northern Hemisphere, you'll experience the longest day of the year on June 21 or 22. This date is when the summer **solstice** takes place.

The shortest amount of daylight occurs in winter. At this time of the year, it might be nearly dark when you get home from school. Look at the picture. On what date does the winter solstice—the shortest day of the year— take place? The summer and winter solstices take place on opposite days of the year in the Southern Hemisphere.

Glossary

Glossary

solstice (sol′stis), a point in Earth's orbit around the sun where daylight is either the longest or the shortest amount possible

Twice a year, an **equinox** takes place when the sun is directly above the equator and the hours of daylight and night are equal. The first day of spring or fall begins on the equinox. You can expect 12 hours of daylight and 12 hours of night on these days.

Earth and the Moon Interact

On many nights when you look at the sky, the most noticeable thing you probably see is the moon. Did you know that the moon is Earth's nearest neighbor in space? Like any satellite, the moon orbits a larger body—in this case, Earth. The force of gravity between Earth and the moon keeps the moon in its orbit around Earth.

As it orbits Earth, the moon seems to change shape and disappear. Actually, your view of the part of the moon that is lit by the sun is what changes. Because the moon and Earth are always moving, the sunlit part of the moon that you can see from Earth depends on the moon's location in space. The shape of this lighted part of the moon that you see is called the moon's phase.

The diagrams show how only the side of the moon that faces the sun is lighted. Notice how at the new moon only the dark side of the moon faces us. As the moon continues around Earth, you start to see a sliver of the lighted moon called a crescent moon. About a week later, when the moon is a quarter of the way around its orbit, half of the lighted side is visible—a first-quarter moon. Next comes a gibbous moon. Halfway around its orbit, the entire side of the moon that faces us is lighted. You see it as a full moon. As the moon continues the second half of its orbit, you see another gibbous, quarter, and crescent phase before the next new moon.

Glossary

equinox (ē′kwə noks), a point in Earth's orbit around the sun where nights and days are the same length

Moon's Orbit

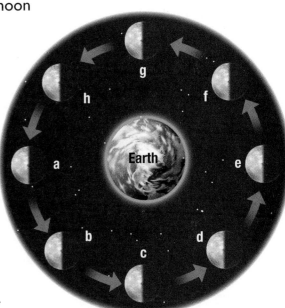

▲ Compare the lighted part of the moon in each position of its orbit (above) to the phase you see from Earth (below). It takes the moon about one month to go through all of its different phases. ▼

Phases of the Moon

| New moon | Crescent moon | First quarter moon | Gibbous moon | Full moon | Gibbous moon | Quarter moon | Crescent moon |

C85

Lunar Eclipse

An eclipse of the moon happens when the sun, Earth, and moon line up. During a lunar eclipse, the moon darkens for as much as an hour as it passes through Earth's shadow. Sometimes light passing through Earth's atmosphere makes the moon look red. ▶

Moon   Earth   Sun

Glossary

Glossary

lunar eclipse
(lü′nər i klips′), a darkening of the moon when it passes through Earth's shadow

tides (tīdz), the rise and fall of water in the ocean and seas caused mainly by the gravitational pull of the moon on Earth

If you did the Explore Activity, you may have discovered how shadows form on spheres. Look at the picture above. Notice how Earth casts a huge shadow in space. Usually the moon passes above or below this shadow as it orbits Earth. Sometimes, however, it passes through the shadow, creating a **lunar eclipse.** During a lunar eclipse, the moon may be partially or totally shaded by Earth. A partial eclipse may happen several times in a year. A total lunar eclipse occurs less often.

The picture below shows another way that the moon and Earth interact. The pulling force of gravity exists among these objects. As the moon orbits Earth, the moon's gravity pulls on Earth's land and water. This gravitational pull slightly changes Earth's shape so that water rises or bulges in two places—the side facing the moon and the opposite side. This bulging causes high **tides**. Lower water levels form between the bulges, causing low tides. As Earth rotates on its axis, the two bulges move to stay in line with the moon.

Low tide

Earth

Pull of moon's gravity

Moon

High tide   Low tide   High tide

▲ *High and low tides are caused mainly by the moon's gravitational pull.*

Lesson 1 Review

1. What are two ways Earth moves in space?

2. What causes seasons?

3. How do Earth and the moon interact?

4. **Large Numbers**
   How many Earth days does Pluto take to complete one revolution? Write the number in its word form.

What Do We Know About the Sun?

Ahh! The warm rays coming through the window on a chilly morning feel good when you stand in the sunlight. Other times . . . **OUCH!** They make your skin feel too hot. Whether or not you enjoy the sunshine on a given day, you always need it.

You will learn:
- why the sun is Earth's most important star.
- how the sun gets its energy.
- how sunspots affect Earth.

Earth's Most Important Star

About 150 million kilometers away from you, a star gives off light and other radiation that are necessary for life on Earth. Can you guess what that star is? If you said our sun, you're right! The sun is so far away that its light takes 8 minutes to reach Earth. Even so, it's a lot closer than the next nearest star, Alpha Centauri. Light from that star travels at a speed of almost 300,000 kilometers per second and takes almost 4 years to reach you!

Our sun gives us radiant energy. Some of this energy can be seen as the white light of sunlight. Other forms of solar energy, such as ultraviolet light, are invisible. Some of the sun's energy is stored in the form of fossil fuels, such as coal and oil, that are found beneath Earth's surface. We use this stored energy to heat our homes and power our cars.

The sun supplies energy for fuel. How have you depended on the sun today? ▶

Glossary

fusion (fyü′zhən), the combining of less massive elements to form more massive elements

corona (kə rō′nə), a crown of glowing gases around the sun that can be seen during a total solar eclipse

During fusion, hydrogen nuclei combine to make a helium nucleus, some smaller particles, and a great amount of energy. ▶

Currents of rising and sinking gases carry energy from the sun's core to its surface. ▼

Corona

Convection current

Energy

Core

The Sun's Energy

Compared with other stars, our sun is considered a medium-sized star. However, this medium-size star is big enough to fit over a million Earths inside it! Its yellow color tells us that the sun is somewhat cooler than hotter stars that glow blue or white. It is also warmer than stars that glow orange or red. Like any other star, however, the sun is made up of hot gases—mostly hydrogen and helium.

The sun started to shine nearly 5 billion years ago. It still shines today because its core—which you can see in the lower left picture—is about 15,000,000°C! At this super hot temperature, hydrogen atoms move at incredible speeds. Sometimes, particles in their nucleus, the central part of the atom, crash into one another. Because the atoms are moving so fast, the nuclear particles may fuse or stick together to form a single, larger nucleus, as shown below. During this process, called **fusion**, atoms of hydrogen combine to form a new element—helium.

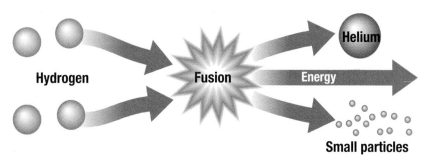

Hydrogen   Fusion   Energy   Helium   Small particles

Stars get all their energy from fusion. When the element hydrogen goes through fusion to create helium, a small amount of the mass is lost. This tiny bit of lost mass converts into a huge amount of energy. Small amounts of this energy reach Earth as sunlight and other forms of radiant energy. Scientists think that fusion will keep our sun shining for another 5 billion years.

Find the **corona**, the thin layer of gases that lies above its surface, in the picture to the left. The sun is so bright that ordinarily you can't see the corona. Gases in the corona are much hotter than the temperature at the sun's surface.

Sun

Moon

Earth

Solar Eclipse

◀ *A solar eclipse takes place when the moon passes between Earth and the sun. (The sun is much farther away from the moon than shown in this picture.) Only people who live where the moon's narrow shadow falls on Earth can see a total solar eclipse—others may see a partial eclipse.*

Corona

▲ *The glowing gases that make up the sun's corona are normally not visible. They can be seen during a total solar eclipse through the use of cameras or special equipment that protect the eyes. The corona's gases expand into space.*

At certain times—such as during a solar eclipse—this outermost region of the sun is visible. You can see above that, during a **solar eclipse,** the moon moves exactly between Earth and the sun. Because the moon is so near to Earth, it appears about the same size as the sun and completely covers the sun's surface. The photo shows how easily the corona can be seen during the eclipse.

Sunspots

At one time or another, you might have experimented with a bar magnet. Did you notice how a magnetic field around the magnet pulled certain objects toward it? The sun has a magnetic field that is similar to that of a bar magnet. The **sunspots** shown below are places where the magnetic field is thousands of times stronger than at other places on the sun. Gases do not move very much in sunspots. These regions are much cooler than the rest of the surface. Since cooler gas shines less brightly than hotter gas, sunspots appear darker than the areas around them. The number of sunspots goes up and down about every 11 years in a period called the sunspot cycle.

Glossary

solar eclipse
(sō′lər i klips′), an alignment of the sun, moon, and Earth where the moon blocks the sun from Earth's view

sunspot (sun′spot′), a region on the sun of very strong magnetic field

Glossary

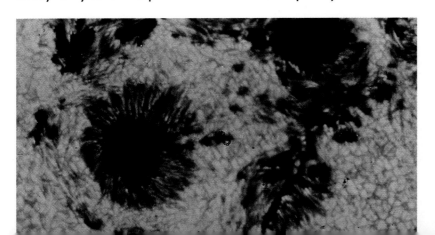

Sunspots

◀ *The dark areas you see in this photo of the sun are regions of cooler gas created from variations in the sun's magnetic field.*

C89

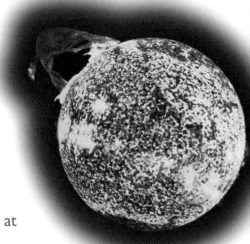

Glossary

solar flare
(sō′lər fler), powerful eruption on the sun

aurora (ô rôr′ə), the glow or display of lights in the skies near polar latitudes

Solar Flares

Temperatures in solar flares can reach 4,000,000°C! Earth's atmosphere usually blocks radiation that escapes from solar flares into space and keeps it from reaching Earth's surface. ▶

Auroras form in the sky over places far north, such as Alaska and Canada, or far south, such as Antarctica. ▼

When the sunspot cycle is at its peak and there are a large number of sunspots, huge explosions occur on the sun. Notice in the picture how these **solar flares** which are many times the size of Earth erupt on the sun's surface. Particles and radiation from the solar flares escape into space and reach Earth's atmosphere. These particles can cause static interference on radios and power surges on electric lines. Blackouts sometimes result from these surges.

Solar flares can cause colorful displays on Earth. The colorful bands or curtains of glowing light in this photo to the left are called **auroras**. The auroras form when particles given off by solar flares hit Earth's atmosphere over the magnetic north and south poles. When the particles hit the oxygen and nitrogen atoms in the upper atmosphere, the atoms sometimes give off a spectacular display of colored light.

Lesson 2 Review

1. Why is the sun Earth's most important star?

2. Explain how the sun gets its energy.

3. How do sunspots affect Earth?

4. **Large Numbers**
   The sun is 150 million kilometers away from Earth. What is the place value of the 5 in this measurement?

Lesson 3

What Makes Up the Universe?

Looking up at a clear night sky far from city lights can be **AWESOME!** You might see thousands of stars. With a telescope or binoculars, you'd see even more. Is that all there is? Not even close! Countless stars and other objects are just waiting to be seen.

What's the Big Idea?

You will learn:
- what galaxies are.
- how stars change during their life cycles.
- what evidence shows that the universe is expanding.

Galaxies

When you look at the night sky, you probably are seeing a lot more than you realize. For example, some of those points of light that you might think are individual stars are actually groups of stars called **galaxies**. All stars belong to a galaxy. Our sun and all the individual stars you can see from Earth belong to the Milky Way Galaxy. Just as planets travel around the sun in a solar system, stars travel around the center of their galaxy.

Scientists classify galaxies by their shapes. You can see the three main shapes below. Spiral galaxies are rotating disks with arms that spiral outward like a pinwheel. The Milky Way Galaxy is a spiral galaxy. Elliptical galaxies are shaped like an ellipse, or oval. Notice that their shape is similar to the center of a spiral galaxy. An irregular galaxy has no particular shape. The nearest galaxies to our own are two irregular galaxies called the Large and Small Magellanic Clouds. The Portuguese explorer Ferdinand Magellan recorded the presence of these galaxies during a voyage in the 1500s.

Glossary

galaxy (gal/ək sē), a system of billions of stars, gases, and dust

Glossary

Types of Galaxies
Spiral galaxies probably formed from giant clouds of rapidly spinning hydrogen gas. Elliptical galaxies are the brightest and largest of the galaxies known. Most galaxies are elliptical. Irregular galaxies have more young stars than the other kinds of galaxies. ▼

Spiral galaxy

Elliptical galaxy

Irregular galaxy

Glossary

quasars (kwā′särz), brilliant objects in space that may be the powerhouses of developing galaxies

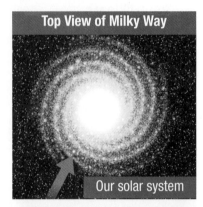

Top View of Milky Way

Our solar system

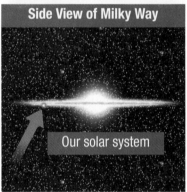

Side View of Milky Way

Our solar system

▲ The diameter of the Milky Way Galaxy is about 100,000 light years.

Our solar system is part of the Milky Way Galaxy. The diagram to the left shows that our solar system is located near the edge of one of the galaxy's spiraling arms. The sun is just one of billions of stars, along with gases and dust, that make up this galaxy.

Galaxies are huge. For example, our solar system is about 30,000 light years from the center of the Milky Way. That means that at the speed of light—300,000 kilometers per second—light takes about 30,000 years to travel from the center of the galaxy to our solar system. Most stars that you can see are at least hundreds of light years away.

Our galaxy is not alone. Galaxies exist in groups called clusters. A cluster can contain hundreds of galaxies. As the drawing below shows, the Milky Way is one of more than 30 other galaxies in a cluster known as the Local Group.

Beyond our Local Group are many distant clusters. Among these distant clusters are **quasars**—extremely bright objects that are thought to be the very active centers of young galaxies. Quasars shine as brightly as a trillion suns and are perhaps about 10 billion light years away. That means their brilliant light started traveling toward us 10 billion years ago!

Our solar system is part of a much larger system of galaxies and space called the universe. ▼

Solar System

Local Group

Milky Way Galaxy

Star Life Cycles

Stars vary in their size, color, and brightness. Astronomers have determined that these differences happen as stars go through different stages during their lifetimes. During its life cycle, a star may appear either red, orange, yellow, white, or blue. A star's color depends on its surface temperature, which is related to the star's age and mass.

The region of gas and dust shown in the photo below is called a **nebula**. This first stage in the life cycle of a star begins when the gas and dust in the nebula are pulled together by the force of gravity. New stars form as pressure from these pulled materials causes the temperature to rise. Fusion begins in the star's core when the temperature reaches about 10,000,000°C. As hydrogen fuses to become helium, hot gases push outward and gravity pulls inward. When the outward push from fusion and the inward pull from gravity balance, a star is born. Energy from fusion reaches the star's surface and shines into space.

Glossary

nebula (neb′yə lə), cloud of gas and dust in space

Glossary

Nebula
Stars are born amid the dust and gas of a nebula. ▼

Glossary

red giant (red jī′ənt), a star that has swelled and glows with a red color

Life and Death of a Star

How long a star lives depends on how long the star takes to use up the hydrogen in its core. Stars that are small or average in mass, such as the sun, shine for about 10 billion years. The most massive stars live for only about one million years because they use up their hydrogen more quickly.

Mid-Sized Stars

A small or mid-sized star like the sun spends most of its life as a yellow star. It glows yellow for about 10 billion years.

Nebula

Red Giant

Once a star has changed all the hydrogen in its core into helium, the outward force caused by fusion no longer balances the inward pull of gravity. The star begins to collapse. Then helium nuclei fuse into more massive elements such as carbon. The energy produced by this fusion expands the star's surface. The star becomes a bigger, cooler red giant. This change won't happen to the sun for another 5 billion years.

Massive Stars

A star that is 10 to 30 times more massive than the sun spends most of its life as a blue star. It glows blue for about 1 to 20 million years.

Supergiant

Like a red giant, the star expands. However, because the star is so massive, fusion continues more steadily. A supergiant forms.

Glossary

supernova
(sü′pər nō′və), the explosion of a star, releasing huge amounts of light and other energy

Neutron Star
Black Hole

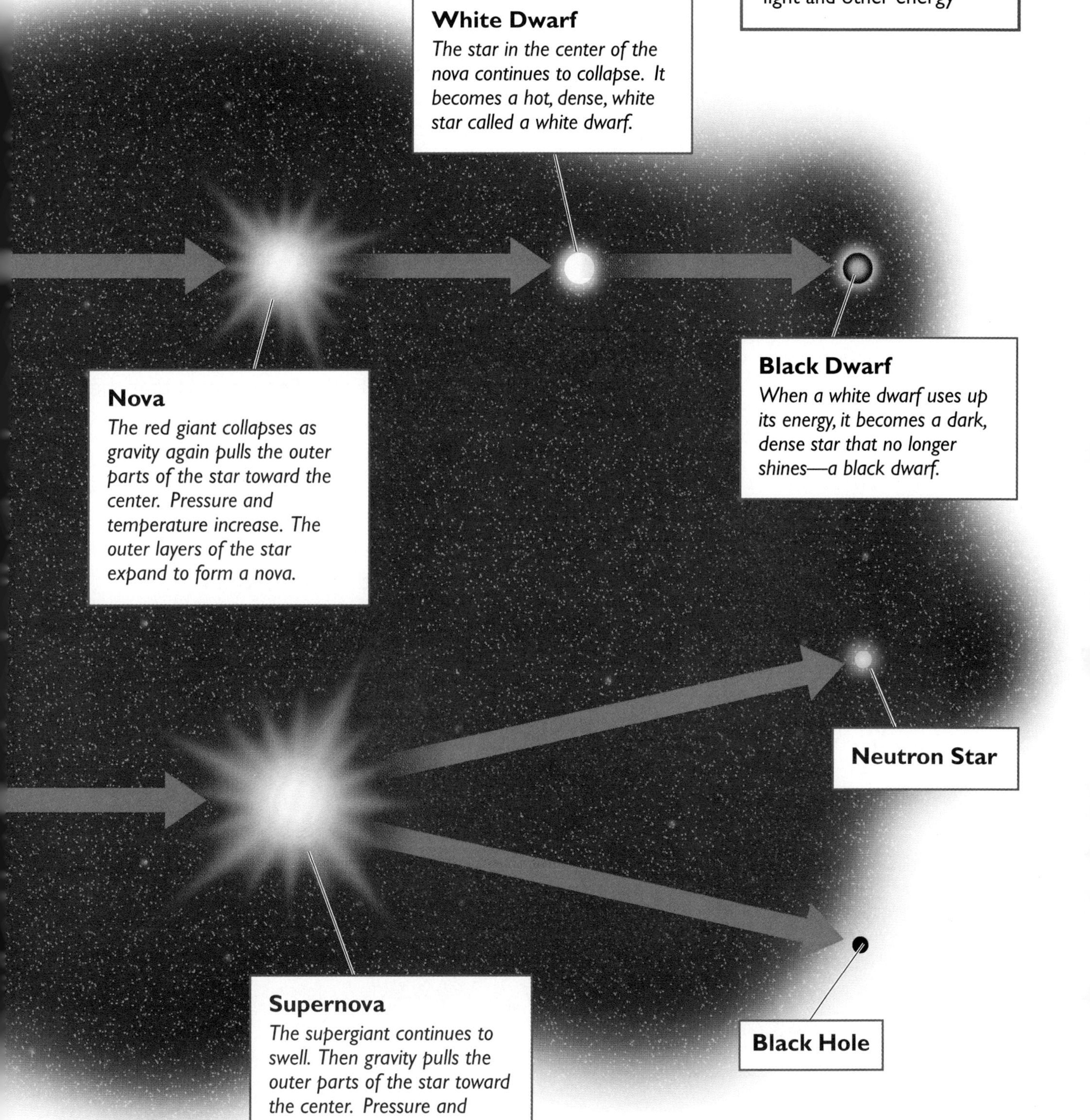

White Dwarf
The star in the center of the nova continues to collapse. It becomes a hot, dense, white star called a white dwarf.

Black Dwarf
When a white dwarf uses up its energy, it becomes a dark, dense star that no longer shines—a black dwarf.

Nova
The red giant collapses as gravity again pulls the outer parts of the star toward the center. Pressure and temperature increase. The outer layers of the star expand to form a nova.

Supernova
The supergiant continues to swell. Then gravity pulls the outer parts of the star toward the center. Pressure and temperature increase so much that the star explodes—a ***supernova*****.**

Glossary

black hole (blak hōl), an invisible object in space whose mass and gravitational force is so great that not even light can escape

The explosion of a supernova may be the most powerful event that occurs in space. During a supernova, a star hurls its outer layers into space at one-tenth the speed of light. Its core crushes down to a compact ball that can't be packed any tighter. The resulting star is known as a neutron star. A neutron star may be only a few kilometers across. Its gases are so compressed that one teaspoonful of a neutron star has the mass of a billion metric tons!

Sometimes the supernova's remaining core is more compressed than usual. Some scientists think this happens when the explosion is so violent that the supernova hurls its material into space at nearly the speed of light. The resulting force of gravity among the gases that aren't hurled into space is so strong that they continue to collapse. Then an invisible object with great mass and gravitational pull, called a **black hole,** forms. The pull of gravity from a black hole is so great that it doesn't even allow light to escape or reflect back. The result is that the light can't be seen.

If no light escapes from a black hole, how do scientists know they exist? Scientists observe the behavior of visible stars that may be near a black hole. They think the black hole pulls gases from the visible star. This pulling away of the gases produces strong, continuous X rays, which astronomers can detect.

Find the black hole in the middle of the disk in this artist's drawing. The disk is made of matter that the black hole's gravity pulls from a nearby visible star. ▼

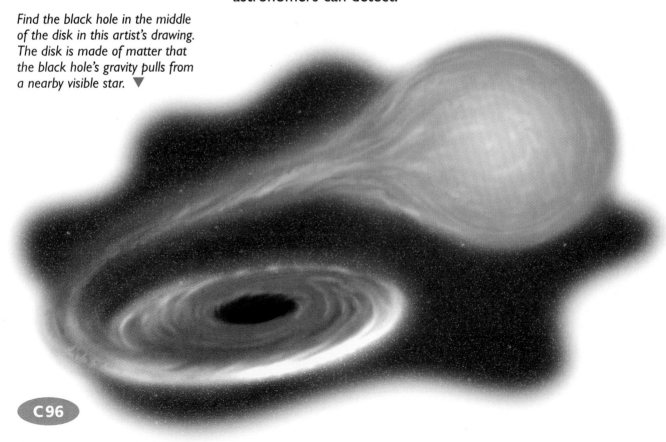

The Expanding Universe

Do you have photos of yourself when you were younger? How have you changed? Earth, too, has changed since it was born. How do scientists know this?

Scientists have developed many theories to explain the universe's history. Today, most scientists think the universe began as a huge explosion—or big bang—about 15 billion years ago. This explosion sent matter and energy traveling through space. The **big bang theory** states that the universe has been expanding ever since.

What proof do scientists have that the universe is expanding? Their proof is in the color of the light that stars give off. To help you understand this proof, think about the sound you would hear as a car passes blowing its horn. The sound has a higher pitch when the car moves toward you and a lower pitch when it moves away.

Just as sound from a moving object changes pitch, light from a moving object changes color. The color change depends on whether the object is moving toward or away. By observing light from distant objects, scientists can tell what direction the object is moving—toward or away from Earth.

Notice the visible light spectrum. When a distant object moves away from Earth, its color shifts toward the red end of the spectrum. Scientists have observed light waves from distant galaxies and found that light from all galaxies is shifted toward the red end of the spectrum. The greater this **red shift** is, the farther away the object is. This red shift tells scientists that galaxies are moving away from Earth and that the universe is expanding.

Lesson 3 Review

1. What are galaxies?

2. How do the stars change during their life cycles?

3. What evidence shows the universe is expanding?

4. **Context Clues**
   Use context clues to write a definition of the phrase *light year* on page C92.

Glossary

big bang theory (big bang thē′ər ē), the idea that the universe started a huge explosion about 15 billion years ago

red shift (red shift), the change of light waves from retreating objects to the red end of the spectrum

▲ Scientists use shifts in color toward the red end of the spectrum to tell that galaxies are moving away from Earth.

Making a Model of the Expanding Universe

Process Skills

- making and using models
- estimating and measuring
- observing
- collecting and interpreting data
- inferring

Materials

- 2 pens of different colors
- large round balloon
- metric tape measure
- safety goggles
- string

Getting Ready

In this activity, you will make a model of the expanding universe.

Measuring will be easier if you keep all your dots on one side of the uninflated balloon.

Follow This Procedure

1 Make a chart like the one shown. Use your chart to record your observations.

Dot number	Distance between numbered dot and red dot (cm)		
	Empty balloon	Balloon half full	Balloon full
1			
2			
3			
4			

2 Make a **model** of the universe. With a pen, draw one red dot anywhere on an empty balloon.

3 Using a pen of a different color, draw 4 more dots on the balloon. Place the dots at different distances from the red dot. Number these dots *1, 2, 3,* and *4.*

Self-Monitoring

Did I make my dots dark enough?

4 **Measure** the distance from each numbered dot to the red dot. Record your measurements (Photo A).

Photo A

5 Put on your safety goggles. Blow up the balloon halfway and hold it closed with your fingers. **Observe** the difference in the balloon and the positions of the dots.

6 Have a teammate measure the distances between the numbered dots and the red dot. Record your measurements (Photo B).

7 Blow up the balloon to its full size. Hold the opening closed while a teammate ties a string tightly around the neck of the balloon.

8 Repeat step 6.

Interpret Your Results

1. In this model, the red dot represents Earth and the balloon represents the boundaries of the universe. What do the numbered dots represent?

2. Interpret the **data** you collected and recorded in your table. Which of the numbered dots moved the farthest from the red dot?

3. Make an **inference**. Which numbered dot moved the fastest?

Inquire Further

How could you prove which dot moved the fastest? Develop a plan to answer this or other questions you may have.

Self-Assessment

- I followed the directions to make a model of the expanding universe.
- I made **measurements** and recorded my **observations.**
- I described what each of the elements of the **model** represented.
- I **interpreted** my **data** to find out which dot moved farthest.
- I made an **inference** about which of the numbered dots on the balloon moved the fastest.

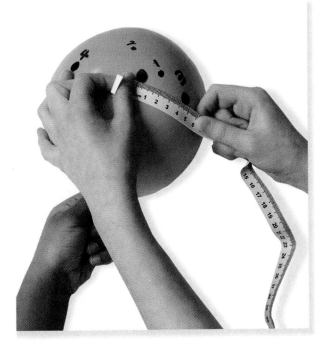

Photo B

You will learn:

- what technology is used to explore the universe.
- how space technology benefits society.
- how space travel has changed.

Lesson 4

How Do People Explore Space?

Let's see . . . one, two, three, four . . . I count ten stars in this part of the sky. Then I look again with a telescope. **WOW!** Where did all those stars come from?! Patches of sky that looked completely black are suddenly filled with pinpoints of light. How did the telescope help?

Exploring the Universe

What do your eyes and the optical telescope in the picture have in common? They both are used to collect light. Scientists all over the world use telescopes to help them learn about the universe. Many of these telescopes look a lot different from the one in the photo below.

The Keck telescope is located on top of Mauna Kea—a large volcanic mountain in Hawaii. This telescope has a total weight of 270 metric tons and is made up of 36 hexagonal mirrors, each about 2 meters wide. These mirrors fit together like tiles on a floor. Each mirror rests on a movable support that is adjusted by a computer twice each second. This constant adjustment enables the mirrors to work together as a single mirror. The Keck telescope is the world's largest light collector. With its great light-collecting power, it is used to look for distant galaxies.

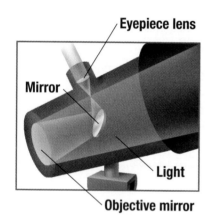

Eyepiece lens

Mirror

Light

Objective mirror

Reflecting Telescope

◀ *A reflecting telescope uses a mirror to collect light. The mirrors of some large telescopes at observatories are 10 meters in diameter. These mirrors collect light from faint, distant objects and focus it in a small area. The larger the mirror, the more light it can collect.*

Observatories are the homes of telescopes. These buildings are built high on mountaintops where the telescopes can get the very best views of space. At these high locations, the telescopes are away from city lights that interfere with the images they collect. The observatory in the photo to the right houses the Keck telescope.

Objects in space not only give off light waves, they also give off other electromagnetic radiation—gamma rays, X rays, ultraviolet waves, infrared waves, and radio waves. Sometimes, these electromagnetic waves coming from space can't easily pass through Earth's atmosphere. For example, light and radio waves can be distorted by the gases in the atmosphere. Some kinds of waves are best studied high above Earth's atmosphere.

Instruments in space can collect information about the universe without interference from Earth's atmosphere. Satellites carry instruments that collect and transmit information about energy in space. In the United States, the National Aeronautics and Space Administration (NASA) is the agency that launches satellites into orbit around Earth.

One of the most important satellites used for exploring space is the Hubble Space Telescope, shown to the lower right. The Hubble was put into Earth orbit in 1990. It has provided views of the universe no one had ever seen before and continues to serve as a useful observatory in space. One important use of this telescope is to help scientists determine the age of the universe.

▲ The Keck telescope, located in this observatory, can collect information about space much faster than other telescopes. It can see deeper into space than other telescopes too.

In 1993, a flawed mirror in the Hubble Telescope was repaired in space. Since then, the Hubble has dazzled people with clear views of deep space, such as the distant galaxies shown here. ▼

C 101

In addition to satellites, scientists have launched space probes. A space probe is a spacecraft without people that leaves Earth orbit to explore space. It collects and sends data about the regions through which it passes. *Voyager, Pioneer, Mariner,* and *Galileo* are some of the earlier probes that have explored our solar system.

A more recent space probe called *Cassini* is shown to the left. It should reach Saturn's moon, Titan, in November 2004. Once there, *Cassini* will drop another probe—*Huygens*—into Titan's atmosphere. *Cassini* will remain above Titan, recording data transmitted by the probe and transmitting the data back to Earth.

A major advancement in the exploration of space has come through NASA's Space Shuttle Program. Space shuttles are reusable vehicles that carry people and equipment into Earth orbit and back. Shuttle astronauts and mission specialists work and live in space for various amounts of time. They conduct experiments, release satellites, and make repairs in space, as shown below.

Longer stays in space are possible with space stations. Early space stations were built by the U.S. and the U.S.S.R. In 1986, the Russian space station *Mir* was launched. Both Russian and American astronauts have lived and conducted experiments in the space laboratory.

Several countries are working together on an international space station. When it is completed, scientists will continue to conduct new experiments in space.

What are some advantages of using space probes such as Cassini *to explore the solar system rather than using astronauts?* ▼

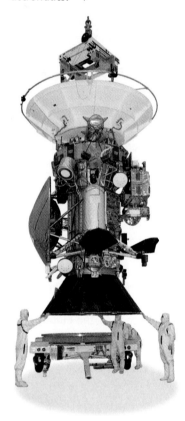

Astronauts Kathryn Thornton and Thomas Akers practice skills that will be necessary for constructing a space station in orbit. ▶

Technology from Space Exploration

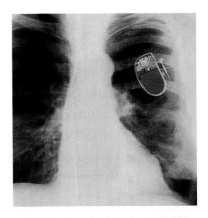

Is your home one of the millions that has its very own Earth station? It is if you receive your TV signals with a satellite dish. Satellites developed for space exploration have many other practical uses on Earth. For example, certain satellites keep track of changing weather conditions for the National Weather Service. Other satellites carry telephone signals around the world. These signals allow the girl in the photo below to use her cellular phone. Some satellites can even track small, special radios on the ground below to help find missing aircraft.

The pacemaker shown on the right is just one of many medical benefits provided by space technology. Portable medical equipment, monitoring devices, implantable heart pumps, and pacemakers all had their roots as equipment designed for use in space.

Chances are, every day you use something that resulted from the exploration of space. The silicon chip used in home computers and calculators is another useful product, or spinoff, that has resulted from space research and exploration.

▲ Technology developed for space programs has led to many medical benefits, including smaller and improved pacemakers that help the heart pump correctly.

It would be hard to escape all the space technology that has found its way into everyday life. Smoke detectors, microwave ovens, and computer bar codes are often taken for granted, but they are all space spinoffs. Some spinoffs came from technology developed to protect astronauts from temperature extremes in space. Some items, such as bullet-proof vests, came from technology developed to provide strong, lightweight fabrics for space use.

Space technology has led to the development of cellular phones. ▶

History of Space Travel

The door opened to space travel in 1957 when the former Soviet Union launched the satellite *Sputnik*. A few years later, the great race to put a person on the moon was on! NASA used increasingly powerful rockets to place astronauts into orbits and eventually on the moon. The Russian space program concentrated on living in Earth's orbit for long periods. The space race eventually changed into cooperative international missions that continue today.

1957
The former Soviet Union launched Sputnik, the first artificial satellite, into Earth orbit. This technological triumph challenged the United States to begin its own space program. On October 1, 1958, the National Aeronautics and Space Administration (NASA) officially began efforts to explore space.

1965
Ed White became the first American to walk in space—an important task for making repairs in space.

1961
In his round capsule, Russian cosmonaut Yuri A. Gagarin became the first person in space. A Redstone rocket boosted the first American into space—Alan B. Shepard.

1981
The first launch and safe return of the space shuttle Columbia in 1981 marked the beginning of a new space era. Space shuttles enable people to do a variety of research and to work in space.

1969
Neil Armstrong and Edwin Aldrin, during the Apollo 11 mission, became the first people to walk on the moon. Michael Collins orbited in the waiting spacecraft overhead.

2000 and Beyond
Scientists, engineers, and astronauts from many countries are cooperating to plan the further exploration and use of space. Future international missions include a large space station that will orbit Earth and a possible mission to Mars.

Lesson 4 Review

1. What technology is used to explore the universe?
2. How does space technology benefit society?
3. How has space travel changed since the launch of *Sputnik*?
4. **Using Graphic Sources**
   Use the picture on page C100 to write a few sentences that explain how a telescope works.

Chapter 3 Review

Chapter Main Ideas

Lesson 1
• Earth rotates in a counterclockwise direction on its tilted axis as it revolves in an elliptical orbit around the sun.
• The seasons change as parts of the earth are tilted either toward or away from the sun at different times throughout its orbit.
• Earth, the moon, and the sun interact to cause tides, eclipses, and moon phases.

Lesson 2
• Our nearest star is the sun, which gives us radiant energy.
• The sun is made up of hot gases and gets its energy from fusion.
• Sunspot activity is accompanied by solar flares, which send radiation into space, causing radio static, power surges, and auroras on Earth.

Lesson 3
• A galaxy is a group of billions of stars with gas and dust.
• During its life cycle, a star changes in size, color, and brightness.
• Scientists have noticed that light from distant galaxies is shifting to the red end of the spectrum. This shift indicates that galaxies are moving away in an expanding universe.

Lesson 4
• Telescopes, artificial satellites, space probes, and space shuttles are used to explore the universe.
• Space technology has provided many useful products that we use every day.

• Space travel began with a race to the moon, followed by unmanned space probes, a space station, and space shuttles.

Reviewing Science Words and Concepts

Write the letter of the word or phrase that best completes each sentence.

a. auroras
b. big bang theory
c. black hole
d. corona
e. equinox
f. fusion
g. galaxy
h. lunar eclipse
i. nebula

j. quasars
k. red giant
l. red shift
m. solar eclipse
n. solar flares
o. solstice
p. sunspot
q. supernova
r. tides

1. The longest or shortest day of the year is the ____.
2. During a(n) ____, Earth's shadow is over the moon.
3. During the ____, there's an equal amount of night and day.
4. The powerhouses of developing galaxies are ____.
5. The gas and dust of a beginning star is a(n) ____.
6. A huge, red glowing star is a(n) ____.
7. The pull of the moon's gravity on Earth causes ____.
8. A dense, invisible object in space is a(n) ____.
9. Atoms combine to form new elements during ____.

10. An exploding star is a(n) ___.

11. The idea that explains how the universe started is the ___.

12. The change of a star's color to the red end of the spectrum is ___.

13. The light display in northern skies are ___.

14. Eruptions on the sun are ___.

15. The crown of glowing gases around the sun is the ___.

16. A region of strong magnetic field on the sun is a(n) ___.

17. When the moon's shadow falls on the earth, a(n) ___ occurs.

18. All stars belong to a(n) ___.

Explaining Science

Draw and label pictures or write sentences on a chart that explain these questions.

1. How does Earth move and interact with other bodies in space?

2. What characteristics of the sun affect Earth?

3. How are stars and galaxies related?

4. How is the universe explored from Earth and from space?

Using Skills

1. Earth is 149,598,000 kilometers from the sun. Write this **large number** in word form.

2. Review the information about seasons on page C84. Then write a procedure for an **experiment** to test whether direct light heats an object more than light hitting an object at an angle. Identify the **variables** you will control.

3. **Formulate questions** you would like investigated on a future space exploration mission.

Critical Thinking

1. Kim lives in Michigan, where winters can be quite harsh. Her brother, Chu, lives in Australia. **Apply** what you know about the seasons to help Kim decide whether to visit her brother during her summer vacation, or during her winter break in January instead.

2. Imagine you could travel to a black hole. **Hypothesize** what would happen as you came upon the black hole's strong gravitational pull.

Reduce!
Re-Use!
Recycle!

Who said backpacks can't be made from old tire rubber! Learning to conserve resources is one way of thinking about the things we use. What other things did this girl find new ways to use?

Chapter 4
Resources and Conservation

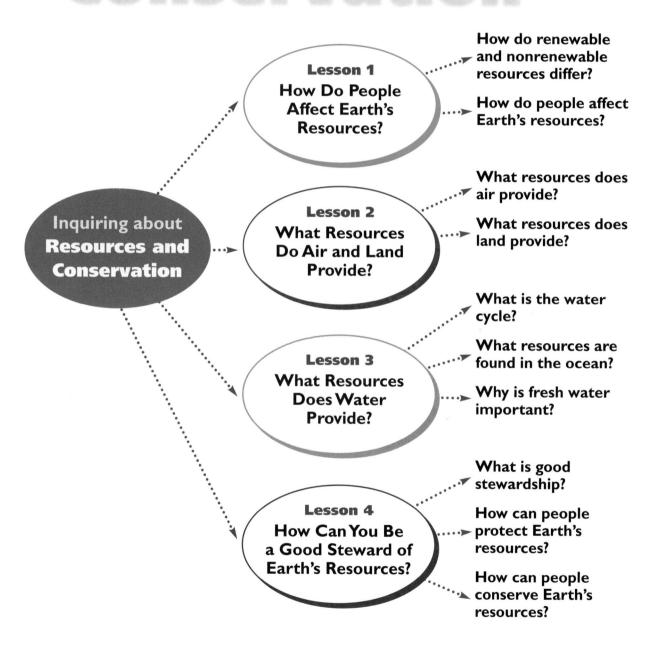

Lesson 1
How Do People Affect Earth's Resources?

How do renewable and nonrenewable resources differ?

How do people affect Earth's resources?

Inquiring about Resources and Conservation

Lesson 2
What Resources Do Air and Land Provide?

What resources does air provide?

What resources does land provide?

Lesson 3
What Resources Does Water Provide?

What is the water cycle?

What resources are found in the ocean?

Why is fresh water important?

Lesson 4
How Can You Be a Good Steward of Earth's Resources?

What is good stewardship?

How can people protect Earth's resources?

How can people conserve Earth's resources?

Copy the chapter graphic organizer onto your own paper. This organizer shows you what the whole chapter is all about. As you read the lessons and do the activities, look for answers to the questions and write them on your organizer.

Exploring Recycling

Process Skills

- observing
- communicating

Materials

- newspaper
- plastic cup
- paper pulp
- foil pan
- window screening
- wood board

Explore

① Cover your desk with newspaper.

② Place 2 cupfuls of paper pulp in a pan. Dip your screen into the paper pulp. Using your hands, spread a thin layer of the pulp on the screen, as shown in the photo.

⚠ **Safety Note** *Be careful not to scratch or cut yourself on the screen.*

③ Place the screen on the newspaper. The pulp should be facing up. Carefully cover the pulp with additional newspapers.

④ Turn the newspaper-screen-pulp sandwich over so that the screen is on top of the pulp.

⑤ Use the wood board to press your pulp, removing most of the water from between the fibers. Turn the screen over so that the pulp is on top.

⑥ Label your screen and place it in a place where it can dry. Let the mixture dry for 1–2 days. Then peel your recycled paper from the screen. **Observe** the recycled paper.

Reflect

1. Describe your recycled paper.

2. Communicate. Discuss the characteristics of your recycled paper with classmates. Make a list of the ways you could test the quality of your paper.

❓ Inquire Further

Your recycled paper is made from shredded newspaper. How would using other materials change the characteristics of the recycled paper? Develop a plan to answer this or other questions you may have.

Comparing and Contrasting

An important part of science is comparing and contrasting events, ideas, or objects. To **compare** things, you identify how they are alike. When you **contrast** them, you identify how they differ. As you read Lesson 1, *How Do People Affect Earth's Resources?* compare and contrast Earth's resources.

Example

You can often use a diagram like the one below to compare and contrast things. Each circle represents a type of resource—renewable and nonrenewable. Fill in each circle with characteristics of the type of resource. When both types share a characteristic, write the characteristic in the area where the circles overlap. One characteristic has been done for you.

Earth's Resources

Renewable Resource

1. Can be replicated in a short time

Nonrenewable Resource

Talk About It!

1. How does comparing and contrasting help you understand what you read?

2. How could you use a similar diagram to compare and contrast three objects?

You will learn:
- how renewable and nonrenewable resources differ.
- how people affect Earth's resources.

How Do People Affect Earth's Resources?

You wake up. **AH!** You take a deep breath of fresh air. **ZAP!** The electricity flows when you turn on the light. Then **WHOOSH,** clean water flows when you turn on the tap. All day and night, you depend on Earth's air, water, and land.

Glossary

renewable resource
(ri nü′ə bəl ri sôrs′), a resource that can be replaced within a reasonably short time

nonrenewable resource
(non′ri nü′ə bəl ri sôrs′), a resource that cannot be replaced

What renewable resource is this girl holding? ▼

Renewable and Nonrenewable Resources

As you go about your daily activities, what are some of the items you use? Food, beverages, clothes, paper, and pencils are just a few of the items you might mention. Any material that makes up the items you use is called a resource. Every item you use is made from one or more resources. Do you know what resources were used to make the items you used today?

The girl to the left is holding items from two groups of resources: renewable and nonrenewable. A **renewable resource** is a resource that can be replaced within a reasonably short time. For example, paper and wood products are made from trees that can be replanted once they have been cut. Food and cotton are also renewable resources because they can be grown or raised by farmers.

A **nonrenewable resource** is a resource that can't be replaced. Many fuels, such as gas and oil, are nonrenewable resources because they take millions of years to form.

Glossary

Because people use gas and oil much faster than they can be replaced, all the gas and oil on Earth will someday be used up. Why is the coal that the girl on the previous page is holding considered a nonrenewable resource?

When deciding whether a resource is renewable or nonrenewable, think about how fast it can be replaced. For example, how much fresh water is available in the area of the country where you live? Fresh water is abundant in the Great Lakes region of the United States. Frequent rainfalls easily replenish the water supply there. On the other hand, water is not so abundant in areas such as the southwest desert where people face serious water shortages. In places like Arizona, the low amount of rainfall can't replenish the amount of water people use.

People Affect Resources

Imagine the enormous hole that an earthmover as large as a 20 story building could dig! The machine shown to the right quickly removes huge amounts of soil and rock, one layer at a time, to expose and remove underlying coal or minerals. An entire hilltop can be removed by this method, which is called open-pit mining or strip-mining.

As people use Earth's resources, there are risks, benefits, and costs. How would you feel if an area near your home was going to be strip-mined? You might not like the big, bare hole that is created as soil, rocks, and plants are removed from a large area. In that case, this use of resources could be considered a cost.

Strip Mining
Gigantic earth moving equipment like the "Big John" strips away layers of soil and rock to remove coal or minerals from the land. In this method of mining, valuable topsoil is buried or washed away. ▼

Strip-mining can have benefits too. It costs less money and is less risky than underground mining. Underground mining can result in cave-ins, gas explosions, and water pollution. The United States government now requires companies to refill strip-mined areas and to plant vegetation. This process is called "reclaiming the land." Reclaiming may be an expensive process, but it is beneficial. Reclaimed land eventually can provide new wildlife habitats or be developed for recreation.

Now think about the risks, benefits, and costs associated with another use of Earth's resources. The photos to the left show some of the effects of building a dam to create a reservoir and provide hydroelectricity. What other impacts might the dammed water have on the area?

▲ Dams, like the one at the top of the page, control the flow of water in flood-prone areas. Although some farmland and forested areas may be lost behind the dam, it provides a a supply of pure water and a place for recreation.

Lesson 1 Review

1. What is the difference between renewable and nonrenewable resources?

2. How do people affect Earth's resources?

3. **Compare and Contrast**
   Compare and contrast the use of resources in your home and in a friend's.

What Resources Do Air and Land Provide?

Have you ever tried to hold your breath for as long as you can? GASP It's not very long before you start gasping for air. People and many animals can't live without air for more than a few minutes. Why is air so important?

You will learn:
• what resources air provides.
• what resources land provides.

Resources in Air

The atmosphere, or air, that you breathe is made up of a variety of gases that you can't see. Nitrogen and oxygen are the two main gases that make up the air. Air also contains smaller amounts of carbon dioxide and other gases. Organisms need these gases to live. Luckily these gases are renewable resources.

In Unit A, you read about the carbon dioxide–oxygen cycle. In this cycle, carbon dioxide and oxygen are continually renewed.

The carbon dioxide–oxygen cycle is part of a larger cycle called the carbon cycle, in which carbon is cycled throughout the environment. Plants take in carbon dioxide from the air to produce carbon-containing molecules. As animals, such as these bison, eat plants, they take in the carbon-containing molecules. When plants or animals die, stored carbon either remains in the ground, or it is released back into the atmosphere as carbon dioxide when matter decomposes.

Nature continually cycles carbon in the environment. ▼

C115

Nitrogen is another renewable resource which all living things need in order to grow and repair cells. Nitrogen gas can't be taken directly from the air. In the nitrogen cycle, the air's nitrogen is changed into a usable form that organisms can use.

Plants of the legume family include alfalfa, peas, clover, and soybeans. The bacteria in swellings on the roots of these plants change the air's nitrogen into nitrogen compounds that plants use to make proteins. As nitrogen-containing plants and animal wastes decompose, a nitrogen compound is released in soil. Plants can take in this form of nitrogen through their roots. However, some of the nitrogen compound is changed by soil bacteria into nitrogen gas, which goes back into the atmosphere.

You can see another renewable resource that comes from air in the photos below. What do you think the resource is? Windmills such as these use wind to turn turbines that generate electricity.

The energy of the movement of air can be captured by windmills. The huge blades on the windmills to the right help to turn turbines that generate electricity. ▼

Resources on Land

When you hear the word *precious* what comes to mind? Did you think of precious stones or metals such as diamonds or gold? Both are types of minerals. Although not all minerals are precious, all minerals are nonrenewable resources that come from the earth. Generally, minerals are found in **ore**, a type of rock that contains enough of a mineral to be of value. The pictures below show some familiar items that are made from minerals.

Soil is one of the most precious resources of all. People use soil to grow the plants they need to live. As plants grow, they take in minerals from the soil. When the plants die and decay, these minerals are returned to the soil. In this way, soil can be used over and over again. Is soil a renewable or nonrenewable resource?

Another important resource is trees. What uses can you think of for the tree being cut down in the photo? You know from Lesson 1 that renewable resources are sometimes used up faster than they can be replaced. Trees are an example of a renewable resource that must be used wisely. People must care for land resources by preventing soil erosion and by replanting trees that have been cut down.

Glossary

ore (ôr), a rock that contains enough of a mineral to be of value

▲ Trees are an important resource that provides many things we use.

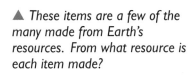

▲ These items are a few of the many made from Earth's resources. From what resource is each item made?

Equally important resources are fossil fuels. **Fossil fuels** include coal, oil, and natural gas. These fuels were formed millions of years ago from the remains of buried plants or animals. Fossil fuels provide energy. Think about the many things you do that require energy. You use energy to cook food, to heat buildings, to drive from one place to another, and to power electrical appliances such as CD players. You can see on the graph that most of the energy that is used in the United States comes from fossil fuels. Smaller amounts of energy come from nuclear power and other sources.

Fossil fuels and the uranium used for nuclear power are nonrenewable resources that are found in the ground. Uranium and coal are obtained by mining. Wells are drilled to obtain underground gas and oil. At the current rate of use, scientists think all the fossil fuels in the world will be used up within a few hundred years. So remember that each time you turn off a light or ride your bike instead of riding in a car, you save fossil fuels.

Energy Production

Nuclear
10%

Other
5.5%

Fossil fuels
80%

Hydroelectric
4.5%

Lesson 2 Review

1. What resources does air provide?

2. What resources does land provide?

3. **Compare and Contrast**
   Compare and contrast soil and air as resources.

Lesson 3

What Resources Does Water Provide?

Rinse the dishes. Bathe the dog. Wash the car. Take a shower. Brush your teeth. Gee! Is washing things all that water is good for? No, in fact, the cells of all living things need water for life processes.

What's the Big Idea?

You will learn:
- what the water cycle is.
- what resources are found in the ocean.
- why fresh water is important.

The Water Cycle

The water cycle provides organisms with a constant supply of the water they need. As you see below, water cycles from the atmosphere to the land and back into the atmosphere. That's why water is a renewable resource.

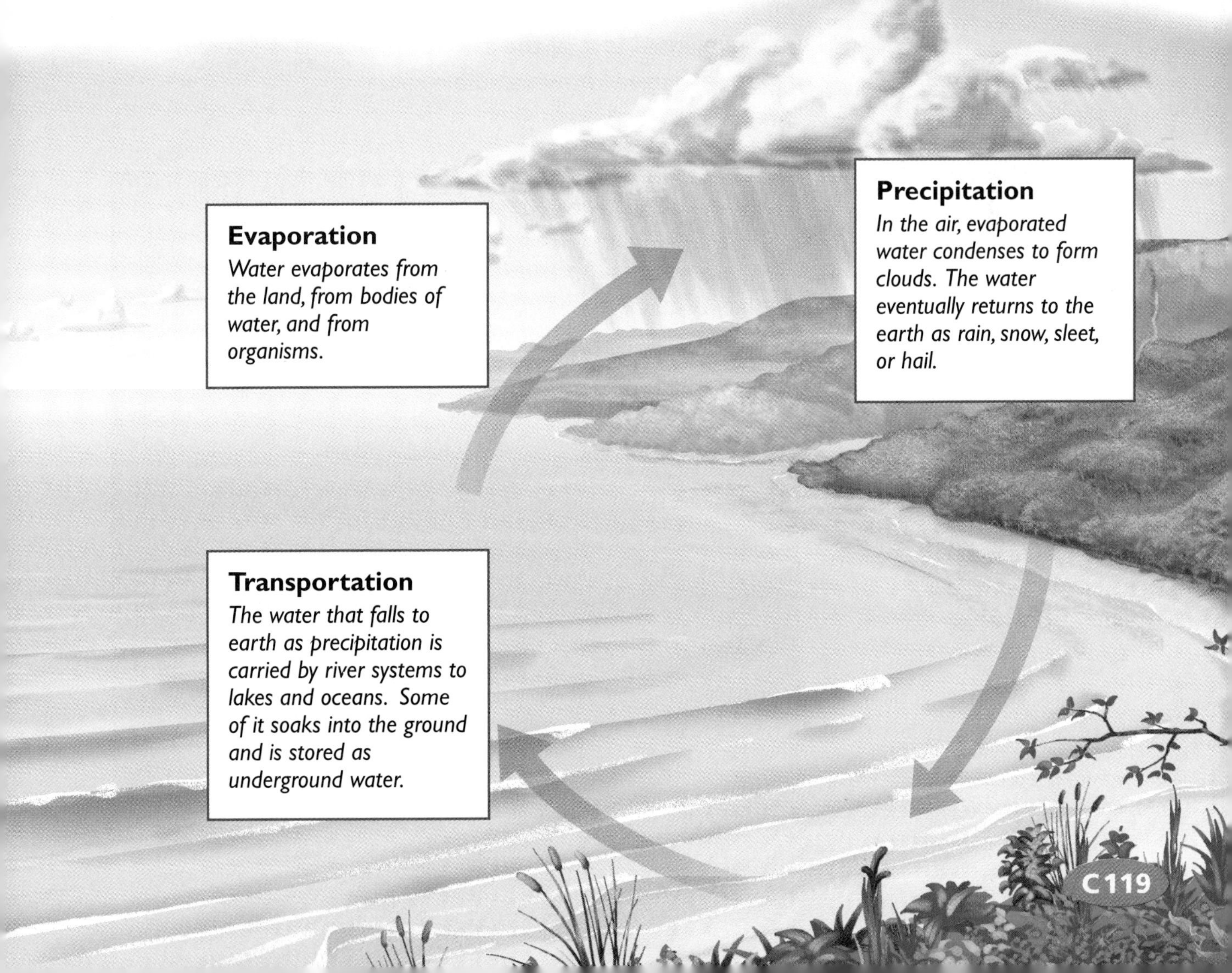

Evaporation
Water evaporates from the land, from bodies of water, and from organisms.

Precipitation
In the air, evaporated water condenses to form clouds. The water eventually returns to the earth as rain, snow, sleet, or hail.

Transportation
The water that falls to earth as precipitation is carried by river systems to lakes and oceans. Some of it soaks into the ground and is stored as underground water.

▲ These nodules on the floor of the Atlantic Ocean are made of manganese.

Ocean Resources

To the left, you see an interesting source of minerals that came from the ocean floor. Each rounded lump of minerals is called a nodule. Minerals such as manganese, iron, and cobalt are found in the nodules. No one knows for sure how nodules formed. The minerals in the ocean water might have collected around a small object, such as a shark's tooth.

Right now, minerals are easier to get from the land than from the ocean floor. However, as minerals on land become more scarce, more will be taken from the oceans. Some people are looking ahead to this time. One machine, a tractorlike robot, has been designed to move across the ocean floor. It scoops up nodules, crushes them, and transports the minerals to the ocean's surface.

Salt is another ocean resource that is found in large amounts. Different types of salts can be obtained from ocean water by evaporating the water. The picture below shows beds of salt that were left by pools of ocean water on the beach. Where pools of ocean water evaporate, the salt remains. Most of the salt in the oceans is sodium chloride, better known as table salt.

Table salt can be removed easily from the ocean by evaporating the ocean water. ▶

In the photo to the right, you see what looks like a miniature chimney on the ocean floor. This opening on the ocean floor is called a **vent**. The black smoke you see escaping from the vent is actually hot water that is rich in sulfur minerals oozing from Earth's crust. If you recall what you know about heat and plate movement, it shouldn't surprise you that vents are commonly found in areas where plate boundaries occur.

When the fountains of hot water rich in sulfur minerals hit the cold seawater, they form crystals that build up around the vent. Many minerals are deposited on the ocean floor around vent openings in this manner. Lead, copper, iron, and zinc are minerals that are found in large amounts near vents on the ocean floor.

Mining these mineral resources from the ocean floor is still too difficult and expensive. Meanwhile, bacteria deep in the ocean use the sulfur minerals that comes from the vents as an energy source. Animals living around the vents then feed on these bacteria.

You might know that oil and natural gas deposits are located under the land. Did you know some of these fuel deposits occur under the oceans as well? Most geologists think that oil deposits formed from carbon in the remains of tiny organisms that once lived in the ocean millions of years ago. These oil deposits are called petroleum or crude oil. Natural gas was produced by a similar process.

To obtain the valuable oil and natural gas resources from beneath the ocean floor, oil wells are drilled into the bottom of the ocean. As you probably can imagine, it is more difficult to drill an oil well under water than on land. Most offshore wells are located somewhat close to shorelines. A diagram of an offshore drilling operation appears on the next page.

vent (vent), opening on the ocean floor

▲ Vents on the ocean floor provide a source of minerals that may be able to be mined in the future.

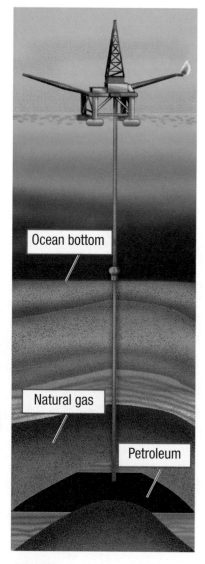

Oil Rig

▲ *Offshore drilling in deep water can be done by drilling ships or floating rigs, like the one above. In shallow water, fixed platforms can be used.*

Ocean bottom

Natural gas

Petroleum

The diagram to the left shows a huge platform that is constructed to support offshore oil drilling equipment. Workers and equipment must be transported by boat or helicopter to these structures, called rigs. In waters such as the Arctic Ocean or the North Sea, storms or floating icebergs can damage rigs, making offshore drilling dangerous for the workers.

Once the oil has been pumped to the surface, it is loaded onto large ships, called tankers. Tankers have huge compartments for carrying the oil to a refinery for processing. Since some tankers can hold as many as one million barrels of petroleum, care must be taken to prevent oil from spilling into the ocean. Oil spills in water can have disastrous effects on plants, animals, and other organisms that live in or near the water.

Oil and natural gas are not the only sources of energy from the oceans. Remember that ocean water moves in regular patterns called tides. The water that moves during tides has much energy. The photo below shows the Annapolis Tidal Generating Station in Nova Scotia, Canada, which is one of several plants that use tidal energy to produce electricity. This plant provides electricity to cities in Canada and the United States. Other tidal power stations can be found in France, China, and the Soviet Union.

Some of the resources from the ocean come from living organisms. Did you use toothpaste, creams, or lotions today? Maybe you enjoyed a dish of ice cream or pudding. All of these items contain a substance that comes from kelp, a type of seaweed that grows in the ocean. The pictures on the next page show many other living resources that come from the oceans.

Tidal Power

This tidal generating station uses tidal movement to turn turbines that generate electricity. ▶

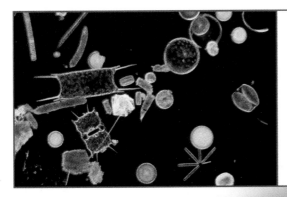

Plankton

◀ Another resource that comes from the ocean are tiny, free-floating organisms called plankton. Plankton includes microscopic organisms such as algae. Algae are a major source of Earth's oxygen as they make food using photosynthesis. They account for up to half of all the photosynthesis that occurs on Earth. Algae are also a major source of food for organisms at the bottom of the ocean's food chain.

Seaweed

Many kinds of seaweed can be eaten. The seaweed in this picture, called kelp, can grow to be 60 meters long. A product extracted from seaweed is used as an additive in cosmetics, toothpastes, medicines, and foods such as jellies or salad dressings. Another product, called agar, from red algae is used to grow bacteria in laboratories. ▶

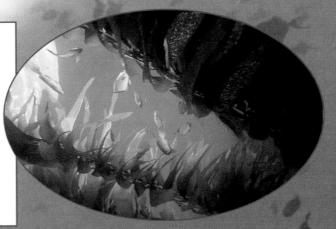

Food Supply

Oceans are a major source of food, including clams, oysters, shrimp, lobster, and many types of fish. Much of the world's population, especially in Asia, depends on fish as the major source of protein. Some of the ocean's fish are processed into fish meal and fed to livestock. ▼

Farm-Raised Seafood

▲ To keep up with the world's demand for seafood, some ocean resources such as oysters and mussels are raised in special containers near shore. Protected from predators, large numbers of sea organisms can grow in small areas and be easily harvested.

Glossary

reservoir (rez′ ər vwär),
artificial lake used to
collect and store water

Fresh Water Resources

Just think about all the water your family uses each day. Each flush of the toilet uses between 13 and 26 liters of water. Taking a 2 to 3 minute shower with the water on full force can use around 75 liters of water. A large load of laundry may use up to 185 liters!

Besides using water for cleaning purposes, you need fresh water—water that contains little or no salt—for your cells to carry out life processes. You might survive weeks without food, but you could not last more than a few days without water.

Fresh water is used to manufacture many types of products. Companies use water as an ingredient in many products or to cool down equipment that becomes hot in the manufacturing process. To make enough steel for a bicycle almost 250 liters of water is used.

Don't forget that animals and plants use water too. For example, cows need more than 10 liters of water to make about 4 liters of milk. It takes as much as 98 liters of water to produce an ear of corn!

Fresh water can be found in lakes, rivers, and groundwater. It is constantly renewed by precipitation that comes from the water cycle. Although some places seem to have plenty of fresh water, the world's available supply of fresh water is less than three percent of all of Earth's water, and it is not evenly distributed. In some places, dams are built to harness a large supply of fresh water in an artificial lake, called a **reservoir**. As you can see in the picture of the irrigated field, in some areas, water is pumped from one location to water crops at another location.

Not only do you need an adequate supply of fresh water, you also need that water to be clean and safe to drink. Places like New York City must provide water for as many as 8 million residents each day. The pictures on the next page show how this might be done. As you study how water comes to you, think about ways you can preserve this valuable resource.

Water is an essential ingredient in food crops. In dry areas farmers may have to water their crops by using irrigation methods, such as the one in this picture. ▼

Supplying Water

Water from distant sources, such as a mountain stream in upstate New York, can be carried by underground pipelines to a location where it is needed. ▶

Large artificial lakes, such as this reservoir in New York City's Central Park, collect and store large supplies of fresh water. The reservoirs are sometimes used for recreation purposes. ▼

Water purification plants process the supply of fresh water to remove many of the impurities. Chemicals such as chlorine are then added to the water to kill harmful bacteria. Special equipment is used to constantly monitor the quality and supply of water. ▶

Purified water is pumped from the water treatment plant to homes, schools, businesses, and playgrounds through a network of underground pipes. The water flowing from the fountain you see pictured here, may eventually find its way back to the reservoir to be recycled. ▶

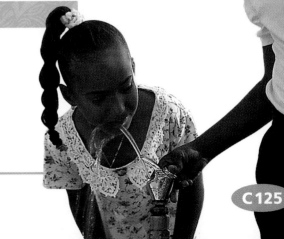

Lesson 3 Review

1. What is the water cycle?

2. What resources are found in the ocean?

3. Why is fresh water important?

4. **Compare and Contrast**
   How is the ocean similar to a farm field?

Purifying Water

Process Skills

Process Skills

- predicting
- observing
- communicating

Materials

- water
- 3 plastic graduated cups
- food coloring
- spoon
- pepper
- cotton balls
- funnel
- coffee filter

Getting Ready

In this activity, you will pollute water and then try to remove the pollutants from the water.

Follow This Procedure

❶ Make a chart like the one shown. Use your chart to record your observations.

Type of filter	Pollutants filter removed	
	Pepper	Food coloring
Cotton ball		
Coffee filter		

❷ Pour 60 mL of clean water into a plastic graduated cup.

❸ Add a drop of food coloring to the water in the cup. Add a spoonful of pepper to the colored water. These materials are your pollutants. Set the polluted water aside.

❹ Place a coffee filter into a funnel. Set the funnel on top of a clean plastic cup (Photo A). **Predict** what will happen if the polluted water is poured through the filter. Will the pollutants be filtered out of the water?

❺ Have one partner hold the funnel in place over the clean cup. Have another partner use the spoon to carefully stir the polluted water in the cup to distribute the pepper and then quickly pour about 10 mL of it into the funnel.

⚠️ **Safety Note** *Stir and pour the water carefully so as not to spill it. Food coloring will stain clothes and skin.*

❻ **Observe** what happens as the water passes through the coffee filter. Record your observations of the filtered water in your chart. Compare a sample of the polluted water with the filtered water.

Photo A

7 Remove the coffee filter from the funnel. Stuff a cotton ball into the thin neck of the funnel (Photo B). If the diameter of the neck of the funnel is not completely filled with cotton, add another cotton ball. Repeat steps 5–6.

Interpret Your Results

1. What did you observe as your polluted water passed through the filter? Was the water slowed down by the filter?

2. Compare the water before and after it was filtered. Were your filters able to remove all of the pollutants?

3. Communicate. Discuss with your group how the results of this activity can be used to explain why chlorine is added to drinking water even after it has been filtered.

Photo B

Inquire Further

What other materials could you use to filter water? Develop a plan to answer this or other questions you may have.

- I followed the directions to filter water.
- I **predicted** what would happen when the water was poured through the filter.
- I **observed** the water being filtered.
- I compared the water before and after it was filtered by two different filters.
- I **communicated** ideas about why chlorine is added to water after it has been filtered.

You will learn:

- what good stewardship is.
- how people can protect Earth's resources.
- how people can conserve Earth's resources.

Lesson 4

How Can You Be a Good Steward of Earth's Resources?

Crash! Sort the glass. **Clank!** Recycle that soda can. **Clunk!** Drop those old phone books into the recycling bin. A community cleanup is just one of the things you can do to help take care of our planet and the resources it provides.

Stewardship

Throughout this chapter, you have seen that people—and all living organisms—can't live without Earth's resources. As in the past, living organisms of the future will also need Earth's resources to live—enough clean air, water, and food. As citizens of planet Earth, it is important to be good stewards of Earth's resources. A steward is a person who is put in charge of property for another.

Using Earth's Resources

| Pre European | 1800s |

Native Americans found a use for every part of the animals they killed. They didn't waste resources. Instead, they took from nature only what they could use or needed to survive.

Many pioneers who settled the West in the 1800s had little regard for the future needs of others. They littered the land and killed buffalo nearly to the point of extinction.

Think about the last time you borrowed a library book. The librarian entrusted you with its care. For a short while, you were the steward of the book. You kept it in good condition so it could be used by others later.

You've also been entrusted with the care of Earth's resources. Just like you, the people born after you will want to live on a planet that is clean, safe, and beautiful. It is your duty as a steward to protect Earth's resources and make sure they will be available in sufficient amounts for future generations. Good **stewardship** means doing what you can to ensure the quality and quantity of Earth's resources for others who will follow you.

As resources are used, good stewards weigh the benefits of their use against the risks involved and make wise judgments. History has shown that people haven't always used Earth's resources wisely. Some people had great respect for nature's gifts. Others mistakenly thought that the supply of resources would last forever. The timeline on these pages shows the way people have used Earth's resources. It shows some events that are leading toward better stewardship. In the sections that follow, you will learn about simple things you can do to be a good steward.

Glossary

stewardship
(stü′ərd ship), the taking care of Earth's resources to ensure their quality and quantity for future generations

1872

The federal government recognized the need to preserve its natural wonders when in 1872 it established the country's first national park—Yellowstone. The National Park Service was established to manage and protect the park's wildlife.

1890

John Muir was an explorer, naturalist, and writer who campaigned for forest conservation in the U.S. His influence led to the establishment of Yosemite and Sequoia National Parks.

Protecting Earth's Resources

At one time, most people lived as farmers or worked as craftspeople who made goods by hand. Then power-driven machines were developed and society changed. The population increased and people flocked to cities to work in factories. Farmland and forests gave way to large urban areas. Chemical fertilizers were used on remaining farmland to produce larger crops to feed the growing population. Exhaust and smoke from cars and factories became common.

As more fuel was burned, air pollution resulted from increased amounts of carbon dioxide and dirty particles being released into the air. Also, waste products were dumped into streams and onto the land. By the 1960s, groups of people began taking steps to fight the harmful substances, or **pollutants**, that were making air, water, and land resources unsafe to use. Pressure from these groups caused the government to pass laws to protect the environment. Since then, companies have also taken voluntary steps to reduce pollution.

Today automobiles have pollution control devices. Treatment plants operated by cities and factories remove human or chemical wastes from water before they are dumped into rivers or lakes. Factories and power plants use devices called scrubbers on their smokestacks to cut down on pollutants being released into the air.

1901	1930	1934

To discourage the waste of natural resources, President Theodore Roosevelt set aside land for national wildlife refuges and forest preserves.

The Civilian Conservation Corps was set up to hire unemployed young men in the 1930s. The CCC planted trees, developed recreation areas, and did other conservation work.

The Migratory Bird Hunting Stamp Act imposed a fee for hunting waterfowl. These and other hunting taxes have been used to buy land for habitat preservation.

It is important for both the nation and individuals to weigh the benefits and risks of actions that affect pollution. Some people are now saying that government environmental standards carry a high price tag. They worry that jobs are being lost to save the environment.

Another environmental debate is going on. More than 20 years ago, some scientists predicted that extra carbon dioxide building up in our atmosphere from human activity would trap more of the sun's heat on our planet. Some scientists have feared that this global warming would result in hot summers, warmer winters, and rising ocean levels. Now some scientists think that the knowledge about global warming is seriously incomplete. They argue that the predicted global warming is not occurring and think that government steps to reduce fuel emissions are not needed at this time.

Regardless of current debates, you can reduce pollution that comes from chemicals you use. Paints, cleaners, glues, and even products like hair spray can cause pollution. You can use biodegradable products that slowly disappear into the soil instead. People can also avoid polluting the environment by disposing of oil and hazardous chemicals properly at special collection sites.

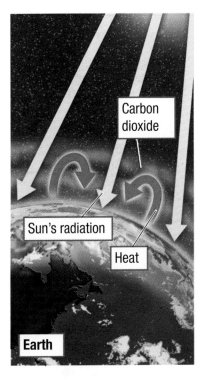

Global Warming
▲ *Some scientists think the huge amounts of carbon dioxide released into the atmosphere by human activity is trapping the sun's heat and causing global warming.*

1948

Twenty people were killed and 6,000 became ill from air pollution at a steel mill in Donora, Pennsylvania in 1948. As a result, people began to question the acceptance of air pollution for the sake of economic progress.

1962

Rachel Carson's book Silent Spring began the environmental movement. The book described pollution from pesticides and other chemicals.

1969

Rivers filled with foam caused by nonbiodegradable substances in detergents increased public awareness of water pollution throughout the 1960s and 70s. This awareness led to a major federal law—the National Environmental Policy Act of 1969 (NEPA).

Glossary

Glossary

conservation
(kon′sər vā′shən), careful use of resources so they will last longer

alternative energy source (ôl tėr′nə tiv en ər jē sôrs), source of energy other than fossil fuels

Conserving Earth's Resources

Not only can resources be polluted, they can also be wasted. If a resource is nonrenewable, it will someday be used up. If a renewable resource is used more quickly than it is being replaced, it too can be used up. When resources are wasted, they disappear even more quickly. **Conservation** is the careful use of resources so that they will last longer.

Fossil fuels are used to make electricity. Therefore, one method of conserving fossil fuels is to reduce the use of energy in your home. Think about all the times you leave the television on when no one is watching. Lights are also left on when they are not needed. What are some other ways you could save energy in your home?

Gasoline can be conserved by riding a bicycle or public transportation instead of using a car. Carpooling is another way of saving gasoline. In carpooling, several people ride together instead of riding in separate cars.

You can also conserve fossil fuels by using other kinds of energy sources, called **alternative energy sources**, to generate electricity. As you learned earlier, in some areas wind energy and moving water can generate electricity. Geothermal energy, energy that comes from hot rock inside Earth, can be used to heat water to steam. The steam can then be used to turn generators.

1970

1970s

The celebration of the first Earth Day in 1970 helped spread public awareness of the need to save the Earth.

The state of the environment began to improve after passage of many environmental laws throughout the 1970s.

Solar energy is another alternative energy source that can be used to heat buildings in some places. Some homes are built so the sun shines in large windows during the winter. These windows are shaded during the summer. Other buildings have solar energy collectors like those on the building to the right that absorb and transfer heat to liquid flowing through pipes in the collectors. The liquid circulates through the building, releasing the heat. Also, solar cells can convert solar energy into electricity. You may have seen solar energy at work if you have ever used a solar-cell calculator.

Use of alternative energy sources may save fossil fuels, but they have limitations. Solar energy or wind power work only when the weather cooperates. Geothermal energy and tidal power work only in places where geothermal or tidal activity are present.

Another alternative energy source is nuclear power. Nuclear power uses the energy that comes when atoms of uranium or plutonium are split in a reactor. Nuclear reactors create electricity without the use of coal or oil. They do not pollute the air as fossil fuels do. However, the water that is used to cool nuclear power systems can cause thermal pollution in lakes or streams. Also, the dangerous, radioactive wastes produced by the reactors must be eventually dispersed into the environment.

Glossary

solar energy
(sō′lər en ər jē), radiant energy that comes from the sun

The sun heats water in coils beneath solar panels on the roof of this home. The heated water provides radiant heating as it circulates through the house and returns to the roof to be warmed again by the sun. ▼

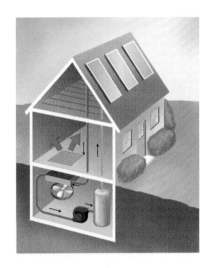

1980	1997	2000+

The pollution of a residential community built on top of the contaminated Love Canal near Niagara Falls, New York led to an increase of money for cleaning hazardous waste sites.

Representatives from different nations gathered in Kyoto, Japan to discuss global warming.

High-mileage electric cars that are virtually pollution-free may be developed as early as 2005. Fuel cells are being developed that use oxygen from the air and hydrogen to produce electricity.

Another method of conserving resources is to recycle them. Newspapers, aluminum, glass, and plastics are some resources being recycled. Some cities provide special recycling bins to homeowners. Trucks pick up the recyclable materials weekly and take them to recycling centers where materials are sorted. Other places have collection sites where people can take recyclable materials sorted at home. If your school doesn't have a recycling plan, you might develop one, like the students to the left.

These students are helping to conserve resources. ▼

Conservation also involves reusing or reducing solid wastes. For instance, instead of throwing away items you no longer use, they can be donated to thrift shops for others to use. You might also want to reduce land pollution by taking part in a community cleanup. Like the students to the left, you can set aside recyclables and take them to community recycling centers. Other trash can be taken to solid waste disposal sites.

Soil is another renewable resource that must be conserved. Wind or water erosion can remove soil that takes hundreds of years to form. To conserve soil, farmers plant crops in ways that prevent water from washing the soil away. They also plant trees along fields to prevent wind erosion.

People can conserve resources in many ways. You can do many things that will make a difference in resources now and in the future.

Lesson 4 Review

1. What is good stewardship?
2. How can people protect Earth's resources?
3. How can people conserve Earth's resources?
4. **Compare and Contrast**
   How has the use of Earth's resources changed in the last century?

Experimenting with Erosion Control

Materials

- 1 qt paper milk carton with one side cut away
- foil pan
- soil
- cup of water
- plastic spoon
- clock or timer
- 2 books
- 2 graduated cups
- newspaper

Process Skills

- formulating questions and hypotheses
- identifying and controlling variables
- experimenting
- observing
- estimating and measuring
- collecting and interpreting data
- communicating

State the Problem

Farmers try to reduce soil erosion and water runoff by plowing the soil in certain ways. Does the method of plowing affect the amount of water runoff from the soil?

Formulate Your Hypotheses

Look at Photos B and C to see two methods of plowing. If you use contour plowing on a hillside, will erosion be less, more, or the same as with terraced plowing? Write your **hypothesis.**

Identify and Control the Variables

The type of contouring is the **variable.** Two plowing methods will be used. Some groups will use contour plowing and other groups will use terraced plowing. Be sure to control all other variables.

Test Your Hypothesis

Follow these steps to perform an **experiment.**

1. Make a chart like the one on the next page. Use your chart to record your data.
2. Place a milk carton on its side, spout down and open, in a foil pan. Add 2½ cupfuls of soil to the milk carton. Slightly moisten the soil with water so that it sticks together and can be molded.
3. Use your hands to pack the soil so that the surface slopes from the back end of the milk carton toward the spout (Photo A).

Photo A

Continued →

Photo B

Photo C

④ Using a plastic spoon, carve indentations into the soil across the width of the milk carton according to your teacher's directions. Some groups will carve terraces (Photo B) and other groups will carve furrows (Photo C).

⑤ Allow the soil to dry for about 30 minutes.

⑥ Use several books to prop up a foil pan. Place the milk carton in the foil pan with the spout facing the lower end.

⑦ Measure 240 mL of water into a graduated cup. When the surface of the soil is firm to the touch, slowly pour the 240 mL of water down the slope of soil in the milk carton. **Observe** the setup while allowing it to remain undisturbed for 3 minutes. Record your observations in your chart.

⑧ Carefully remove the milk carton from the pan and place the milk carton on sheets of newspaper. Pour the water that has collected in the pan into a graduated cup. **Measure** the volume of the water. Record your data in your chart.

⑨ Observe the water's degree of cloudiness. The cloudiness of the water is an indication of the amount of erosion. Rate the water as slightly cloudy, moderately cloudy, or very cloudy. Record your data in your chart.

Collect Your Data

Type of plowing	Volume of runoff	Cloudiness of runoff

Interpret Your Data

1. Combine your data with that of other groups to make a data table. To interpret the data from all the groups, label two sheets of grid paper as shown. Use the data from the group chart to make two bar graphs that show the amount of erosion observed and the amount of runoff measured.

2. Study your bar graphs. Describe what happened in the "fields" with contour plowing compared with fields with terraced plowing. Which method of plowing resulted in less erosion? Which method resulted in less runoff?

State Your Conclusion

Communicate your results. Was your hypothesis supported by the data? Explain how the plowing pattern in a sloping field might affect the amount of erosion and water runoff by the soil. Is one method of plowing superior to the other?

Inquire Further

If you added plants to the soil in the experiment, would the amounts of erosion and runoff increase, decrease, or remain the same? Develop a plan to answer this or other questions you may have.

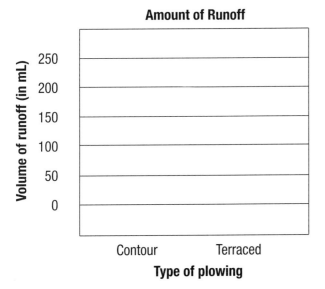

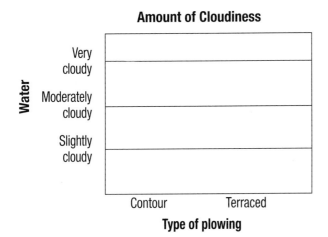

Chapter 4 Review

Chapter Main Ideas

Lesson 1
• Renewable resources can be replaced within a short time. Nonrenewable resources can't be replaced or are used up faster than their rate of replacement.
• Human use of resources can have positive and negative effects.

Lesson 2
• Air provides wind energy, as well as oxygen, carbon dioxide, and nitrogen, which living organisms need for their survival.
• The land provides minerals, fossil fuels, soil, and trees.

Lesson 3
• Water cycles through the land to the atmosphere and back again through the water cycle.
• Ocean resources include minerals, fossil fuels, and tidal energy, as well as living resources used for food and cosmetics.
• Fresh water is used for consumption, cleaning, manufacturing, and agriculture.

Lesson 4
• Good stewardship means doing what you can to ensure the quantity and quality of the earth's resources for others who will follow you.
• Individuals can protect the earth's resources by making wise judgments about resource use and pollution.
• People can conserve the earth's resources by reducing energy use, by using alternative energy sources, by reducing or reusing waste, and by preventing soil erosion.

Reviewing Science Words and Concepts

Write the letter of the word or phrase that best completes each sentence.

a. alternative energy source
b. conservation
c. fossil fuel
d. nodule
e. nonrenewable resource
f. ore
g. pollutant
h. renewable resource
i. reservoir
j. solar energy
k. stewardship
l. vent

1. A tree is an example of a(n) ____.
2. A resource that takes millions of years to form is a(n) ____.
3. Most minerals are found in ____.
4. A fuel that formed from the remains of buried plants and animals is a(n) ____.
5. A source of minerals from the ocean floor is a(n) ____.
6. Water rich in sulfur minerals escapes from an opening, called a(n) ____, in the ocean floor.
7. A large artificial lake that holds a supply of fresh water is a(n) ____.
8. Making sure that future generations have sufficient resources is good ____.
9. A harmful substance that is dumped into a lake is a ____.
10. Using resources in a way that makes them last longer is ____.

11. Geothermal energy is an example of a(n) ___.

12. The radiant energy that comes from the sun is ___.

Explaining Science

Create a poster or write a paragraph that answers each question.

1. How do humans hurt and help the earth's resources?

2. How do people depend on the earth's air and land?

3. Why is water considered a resource?

4. What can individuals do to save and protect the earth's resources?

Using Skills

1. Make a poster that **compares** and **contrasts** the effects of good and poor stewardship of the earth's resources.

2. Formulate questions you might ask a candidate for office to determine if he or she supports stewardship.

3. Collect and interpret data on the use of resources in your classroom or school to determine whether people at your school are good stewards of the environment.

Critical Thinking

1. Suppose a construction company wanted to build a new shopping center across the street from your home. What information would you like to know before you could **evaluate** how you feel about the construction?

2. List three things you can do to be a good steward of the earth's resources. Practice these ideas for one week. Then identify and **solve any problems** you may have had.

3. Sequence the events in the carbon cycle by writing them in numbered steps.

Unit C Review

Reviewing Words and Concepts

Choose at least three words from the **Chapter 1** list below.
Use the words to write a paragraph about how these concepts
are related. Do the same for each of the other chapters.

Chapter 1
air mass
air pressure
barometer
Doppler radar
forecast
meteorologist

Chapter 2
aquifer
fault
focus
groundwater
lithosphere
water table

Chapter 3
auroras
equinox
fusion
solar flares
solstice
sunspots

Chapter 4
fossil fuel
nonrenewable
  resources
ore
pollutants
stewardship
vents

Reviewing Main Ideas

Each of the statements below is false.
Change the underlined word or
words to make each statement true.

1. Relative humidity is the point at which
   the air contains as much water vapor
   as it can hold.

2. Psychrometers are instruments used
   to measure wind speed.

3. A tornado is a large tropical storm
   over warm water.

4. Mountain ranges may be produced at
   a fault boundary.

5. A moraine is a large mass of slowly
   moving ice carrying sediment.

6. The earth takes a year to rotate
   around the sun.

7. During a solar eclipse, the earth lies
   between the sun and the moon.

8. A solar flare is a region on the sun
   with a strong magnetic field.

9. Ores containing precious metals are a
   renewable resource.

10. Conservation means taking care of
    Earth's resources for future
    generations.

Interpreting Data

The relative humidity is obtained by using the difference between temperatures shown on a dry thermometer and one whose bulb is covered by a damp cloth. The table shows the relative humidity at several temperatures.

Relative Humidity Table (shown in %)

Dry bulb	Difference between wet and dry bulb readings (°C)				
°C	1	2	3	4	5
10	88	77	66	55	44
11	89	78	67	56	46
12	89	78	68	58	48
13	89	79	69	59	50
14	90	79	70	60	51

1. If the dry bulb reads 13°C and the wet bulb reads 9°C, what is the relative humidity?

2. If the relative humidity is 55%, what are the wet and dry bulb readings?

3. How do you know that the wet bulb temperature is always lower than the dry bulb temperature?

Communicating Science

1. Write a paragraph explaining the relationships among air pressure, air temperature, and relative humidity.

2. Draw a diagram and write a paragraph that explains how and why the soil profile in various parts of the country may be different.

3. Draw and label a diagram showing how it can be summer at one location on the earth while it is winter at another location.

4. Make a table that gives examples of renewable and non-renewable resources from air, water, and land.

Applying Science

1. Write a paragraph describing the major weather conditions shown on the weather map below.

2. Write a diary entry about what it would be like to live on a space station. Try to include activities that you do in everyday life. Describe how these activities are different on the space station.

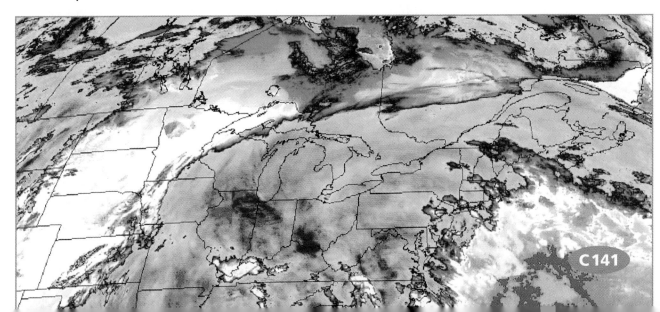

Unit C
Performance Review

Planetarium

Using what you learned in this unit, help prepare exhibits and presentations for an Earth in the Universe Day to be held in your school. Complete one or more of the following activities. You may work by yourself or in a group.

Role-Playing

Working with other students, perform a demonstration showing how the phases of the moon are produced and observed. Have a student with a flashlight play the sun, another the earth, and another the moon. Plan how you will move so that an observer will understand why we see different moon phases during the month. Have a student narrate the demonstration.

Art

Make and label clay models showing the similarities and differences among fault boundaries, spreading boundaries, and colliding boundaries. Display your models with pictures of locations on Earth where such boundaries exist. Be prepared to explain your models.

Mathematics

Prepare a scale model of the solar system. You will need to know the distances between the planets and the sun. Draw the planets in a way as to indicate their relative sizes.

Stewardship

Find out what stewardship efforts are being made in your community. Include efforts by government, industry, agriculture, or groups of concerned citizens. Organize a group of students to participate in one or more of the existing activities or develop one of your own.

Music

Research music, both classical and popular, written about stars and planets. For example, in a suite of music by Gustav Holst called *The Planets,* each of the seven movements is related to one of the planets. Find a number of songs about the sun, moon, stars, and planets. Plan a narration that ties the music together and prepare a presentation.

Using Reference Sources

You can use many different kinds of reference sources to do research. For example, to find the meaning of a word you may look in a dictionary. If you want to learn more about something you studied in school, you may read a book, an encyclopedia entry, or a newspaper or magazine article.

A great deal of information can be found on the World Wide Web. The National Aeronautics and Space Administration (NASA) has a popular Web site that provides a great deal of information about the exploration of space.

Go On-Line

In Chapter 3, you learned about some of the ways people explore space. To learn more about the history of the American space program, use a computer to contact the NASA Web site at the following address: http://www.nasa.gov.

As you surf through the site, list the names and dates of five space missions in which NASA has participated. Include details about the type of spacecraft used for each mission and a brief description of each mission's goals. If you need more information about a mission that interests you, try contacting NASA by e-mail to find what you need.

Write a Summary

Review the information you found on-line. Use this information to write a summary about two space missions you found particularly interesting. Be sure to include a main idea sentence and supporting details in each paragraph of your summary.

Remember to:

1. **Prewrite** Organize your thoughts before you write.

2. **Draft** Make an outline and write your summary.

3. **Revise** Share your work and then make changes.

4. **Edit** Proofread for mistakes and fix them.

5. **Publish** Share your summary with your class.

Your Science Handbook

⚠ **Safety in Science**   2

Using the Metric System   4

Science Process Skills Lessons

   Observing   6

   Communicating   8

   Classifying   10

   Estimating and Measuring   12

   Inferring   14

   Predicting   16

   Making Operational Definitions   18

   Making and Using Models   20

   Formulating Questions
   and Hypotheses   22

   Collecting and Interpreting Data   24

   Identifying and
   Controlling Variables   26

   Experimenting   28

Science Reference Section   30

Ⓗ **History of Science**   44

Glossary   56

Index   65

⚠ Safety in Science

Scientists know they must work safely when doing experiments. You need to be careful when doing experiments too. Here are some safety tips to remember.

Safety Tips

- Read each experiment carefully.
- Wear safety goggles when needed.
- Clean up spills right away.
- Never taste or smell substances unless directed to do so by your teacher.
- Handle sharp items carefully.
- Tape sharp edges of materials.
- Handle thermometers carefully.
- Use chemicals carefully.
- Dispose of chemicals properly.
- Put materials away when you finish an experiment.
- Wash your hands after each experiment.

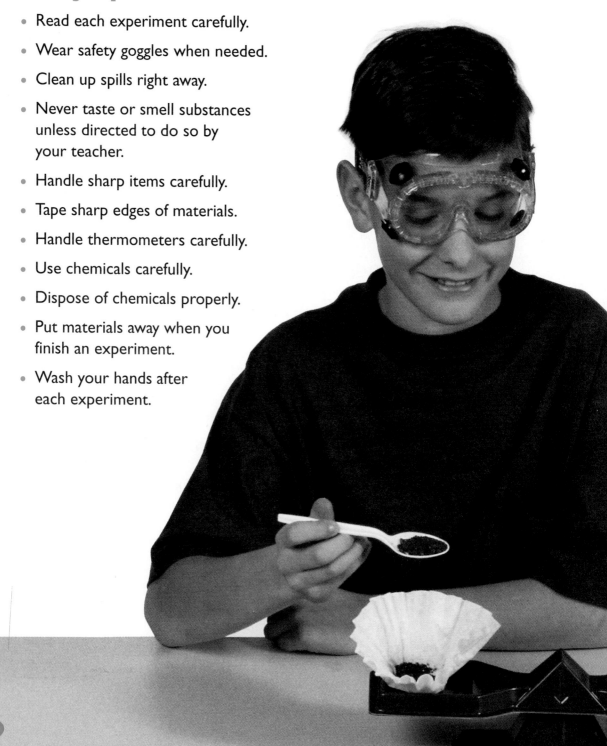

Using the Metric System

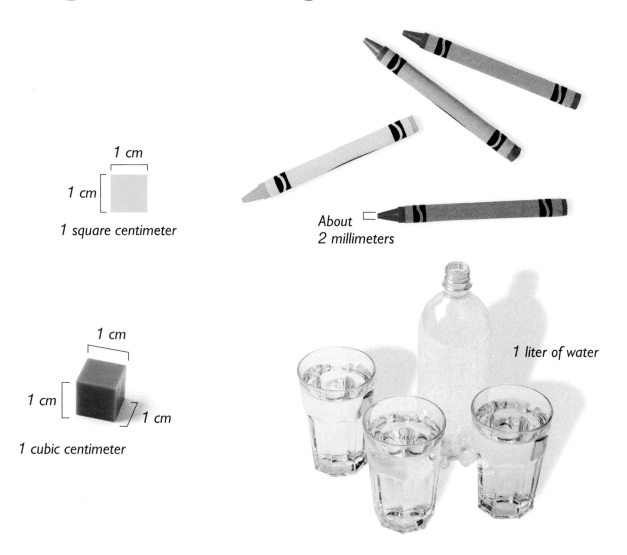

1 cm

1 cm

1 square centimeter

About
2 millimeters

1 cm

1 cm

1 cm

1 cubic centimeter

1 liter of water

11 football fields end to end
is about 1 kilometer

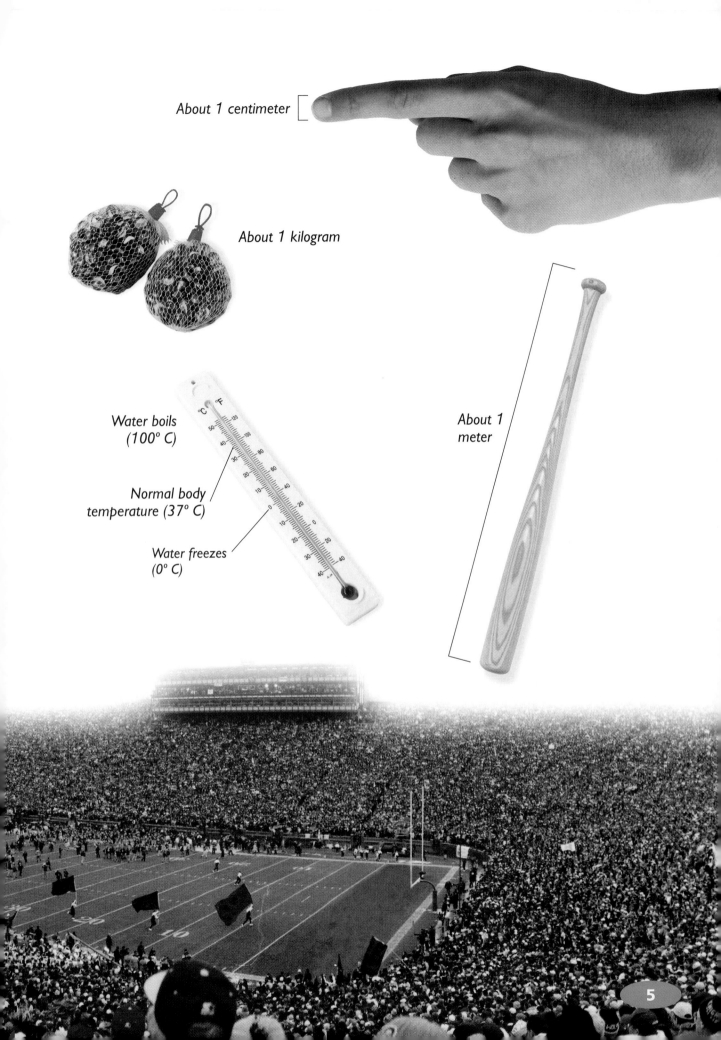

About 1 centimeter

About 1 kilogram

Water boils
(100° C)

Normal body
temperature (37° C)

Water freezes
(0° C)

About 1
meter

5

Observing

How can you increase your powers of observation?

Using your senses helps you understand and learn about the world around you. For example, imagine picking up a ball. Think about the texture. Is it soft, hard, or a combination of both of these things? Does smelling the ball tell you if it is made of plastic or rubber? Imagine shaking it. Is it solid or hollow? Can you tell if something is inside the ball? Are there any characteristics about the ball that can help you determine whether or not the ball can bounce?

As a result of careful observations, you will understand how things and events change. This understanding allows you to make accurate comparisons. Every observation you make is an important one.

Practice Observing

Materials

- box of unshelled peanuts
- marker
- index card
- metric ruler
- hand lens

Follow This Procedure:

1. Choose a peanut from the box.

2. Use a marker to place a small identifying mark on the peanut. Do not share your mark with other students.

3. Observe your peanut carefully. Record as many observations about your peanut as you can on an index card. Be specific.

4. When you've finished observing your peanut, place it back into the box.

5. Exchange your observation card with a classmate. Use the observations on the cards to identify each other's peanuts.

Thinking About Your Thinking

What senses did you use to observe your peanut? Did your partner use observations similar to those you used? What additional observations could you have recorded to better describe your peanut?

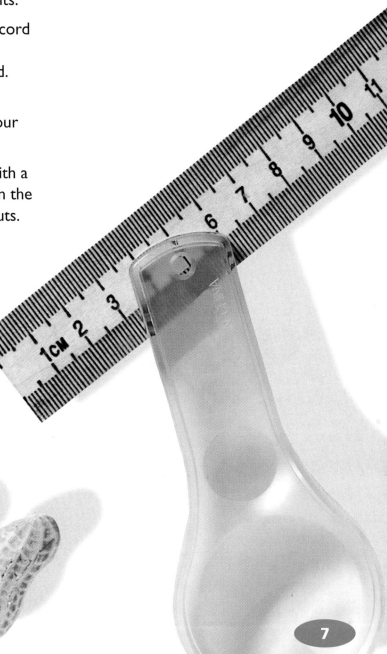

Communicating

How can you communicate in an effective and easily understood way?

Good scientific communication uses words, pictures, charts, and graphs to give information that it is easily understood by people all around the world.

When you make and record observations, it is important to use exact words and to give as much information as possible. Compare the following observations that two students wrote after they observed the same experiment.

The liquid changed color and bubbles formed.

The liquid changed from pale yellow to bright red. Bubbles began forming almost immediately. The liquid bubbled rapidly for 27 seconds and then stopped.

The second student's observations are more exact and complete. Anyone reading these observations can get a fairly good idea of what the student observed. This is not true of the first student's description. The second student communicated in a more meaningful way.

Practice Communicating

Materials

- box of cards with pictures on them
- colored pencils
- 2 sheets of drawing paper

Follow This Procedure

1. Work with a partner. Choose a picture card from the box. Don't show the card to your partner.

2. Look at the picture on your card. Think how you would describe the picture to another person. Where would you start? What words would you use?

3. Slowly and carefully describe the picture on your card to your partner. As you describe the picture, your partner should draw what you describe.

4. When you've completed your description, compare your partner's drawing to the picture on the card. How well did you communicate what you saw?

5. Reverse roles and repeat steps 1–4.

Thinking About Your Thinking

What process did you use to describe your picture? What part did you describe first? Why did you decide to start with that part of the picture? How could you have communicated your information more clearly?

Classifying

How can you classify objects?

Classifying is the process of organizing or arranging objects into groups according to characteristics they share. You classify objects in order to organize your thoughts and knowledge about a subject. This organization of information helps you better understand the objects and events you observe.

What characteristics do the birds on this page share? Based on these similarities, the canary and the duck are both classified as birds. With this information, you can make generalizations about these animals based on your knowledge of the bird group. For example, you can conclude that the canary and the duck lay eggs because egg laying is a characteristic shared by all birds.

In order to classify objects, you must be able to recognize the characteristics that are similar or different among a group of objects. Then you can group the objects according to one or more of their similar characteristics.

Practice Classifying

Materials

- paper
- pencil
- buttons

Follow This Procedure:

1. Observe a group of buttons. Notice how the buttons are similar and how they are different. Record your observations on a sheet of paper.

2. Choose one characteristic. You might choose size, shape, color, or any other characteristic. Based on this characteristic, classify the buttons into two different groups. Record the characteristics each group shares.

3. Now classify each group into various smaller groups based on other similar characteristics. How are the buttons in each group similar? How are they different? Record the characteristics of each group.

4. Report your group's classification to the class. Discuss how the classifications differed among the groups.

Thinking About Your Thinking

The same objects can be classified differently by different people. Why do you think this might occur? Support your answer with some examples.

Estimating and Measuring

How can you accurately estimate and measure?

An estimate is an intelligent guess about an object or an event. One common characteristic that people estimate is measurement. As you get more practice measuring objects, you should find that making estimates that are very close to actual measurements becomes easier.

Being able to estimate volume is often helpful as you do science experiments. Estimating volume can be difficult if an object is irregularly shaped, such as the pebbles below. However, by finding the volume of one pebble, you can better estimate the volume of the other three.

Practice Estimating and Measuring

Materials

- 50-mL plastic graduated cylinder
- water
- 4 irregularly-shaped pebbles of varying sizes

Follow This Procedure

1. Copy the chart onto a sheet of paper. Use your chart to record your observations.

2. Fill a graduated cylinder with water to the 25-mL mark.

3. Choose the pebble that you think has the smallest volume.

4. Estimate the level to which you think the water will rise if you place the pebble into the cylinder. Record your estimate.

5. Gently place the pebble in the water. Record the level of the water in the cylinder.

6. Compare your estimate of the water level to the actual measurement. Are you surprised by the new water level?

7. Find the volume of the pebble by subtracting 25 mL from the actual level of water. Record this volume.

8. Repeat steps 4–7 until you have estimated and measured the volume of all four rocks.

Thinking About Your Thinking

Do you think it will be easier to predict the volume of a regularly-shaped object such as a marble than it is to predict the volume of an irregularly-shaped object? Why or why not?

Pebble	Estimated level of water	Actual level of water	Volume of pebble
1			
2			
3			
4			

Inferring

How can you make a valid inference?

When you make an inference, you make a reasonable guess about information that is not obvious. An inference is based on observations and past experience. In order to make an inference, you must make good observations and consider all the information you have about a situation. Think about how what you've observed relates to situations you are familiar with.

Inferring is an important first step toward predicting outcomes of experiments and forming testable hypotheses. Although an inference must be based on observations or facts, it doesn't always have to be true. After further investigation and experimentation, you might discover that your original inference missed the mark. If necessary, you can make another inference based on the new information you gathered.

Practice Inferring

Materials

- safety goggles
- spoon
- baking soda
- 3 small plastic cups
- hand lens
- dropper
- 3 unknown substances marked A, B, and C
- vinegar

Substance	Observations Without Vinegar	With Vinegar
Baking soda		
Unknown A		
Unknown B		
Unknown C		

Follow This Procedure

1. Copy the chart onto a sheet of paper. Use your chart to record your observations.

2. Put on your safety goggles. Place a half spoonful of baking soda in a plastic cup. Observe the baking soda with a hand lens. Record your observations.

3. Repeat step 2 with the unknown substances.

4. Make an inference. Based on your observations, which substances are baking soda? Record your inference on your paper.

5. Use the dropper to add three drops of vinegar to the cup with the baking soda. Observe what happens. Record your observations in your chart.

6. Repeat step 5 with Unknowns A–C.

7. Review your inferences from step 4. If necessary, make new inferences based on your observations.

Thinking About Your Thinking

What information from this activity did you use to make your inferences? What information from past experiences did you use? How did making additional observations affect your inferences?

Predicting

How can you improve your predicting skills?

When you make a prediction, you guess what will happen in a particular situation. Your prediction is based on knowing what has happened in similar situations. The more information you have and the better your observations, the more likely you are to make accurate predictions.

Look at the cars and ramps below. What amount of force is needed to pull the car up the ramp in the first two pictures? How does this force relate to the height of the ramp?

Now, use the information from the first two photos to predict the amount of force needed to pull the car up the third ramp. Based on your observations of the first two pictures, you can predict that the force needed is three times that in the first picture, or 75N.

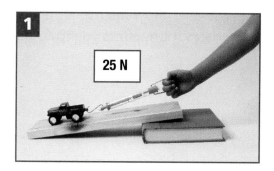

25 N

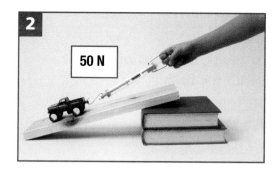

50 N

Practice Predicting

Materials

- feather
- book

Follow This Procedure:

1. Copy the chart onto a sheet of paper. Use your chart to record your predictions and observations.

2. Hold a book in one hand and a feather in the other. If you drop both at the same time, which will reach the ground first? Record your prediction in your chart.

3. Drop the two items. Record your results.

4. Place the feather on top of the book. If you drop the book with the feather lying on top, which will reach the ground first, the feather or the book? Record your prediction.

5. Drop the book with the feather on top of it. Record your results.

	Prediction	Observation
Feather and book dropped separately		
Book dropped with feather on top		

Thinking About Your Thinking

What information did you use to make your prediction in step 2? in step 4? What additional information would have helped you make better predictions?

Making Operational Definitions

How can you make an operational definition?

An operational definition is a definition or description of an object or an event based on the way you experience it.

An operational definition can describe many different qualities of an object or an event. It can explain what something does, what purpose something serves, or how an event takes place.

For example, look at the pictures below which show a strip of litmus paper that has been dipped into some vinegar. The pictures show that when the blue litmus paper is dipped into vinegar, which is an acid, it turns red. Based on this test, an operational definition for an acid might be "a substance that turns blue litmus paper red."

Practice Making Operational Definitions

Materials

- slice of potato
- paper towel
- dropper
- iodine solution
- slice of carrot
- small cup of water
- saltine
- piece of cooked egg white

Food Item	Starch?	Color when iodine is added
Potato	yes	
Carrot	yes	
Water	no	
Saltine	yes	
Egg white	no	

Follow This Procedure

1. Copy the chart onto a sheet of paper. Use your chart to record your observations.

2. Place a slice of potato on a paper towel.

3. With the dropper, place a small drop of iodine solution on the potato. Observe what happens to the potato. Record your observations in your chart.

4. Repeat steps 2 and 3 with the remaining food items.

5. Look up the definition for the word *starch* in a dictionary. Write the definition on your paper below your chart.

6. Look in the chart to see which items contain starch. Use that information and the results of this activity to write an operational definition of a starch.

Thinking About Your Thinking

How is your operational definition different from the definition of a starch in the dictionary? When might your operational definition be more useful than the dictionary definition?

19

Making and Using Models

How do scientific models help you understand science?

A scientific model can be an object or an idea that shows how something that you can't observe directly looks or works. Using models allows you to better understand objects, events, or ideas. Good models can be used to explain what you know and to predict what will happen.

The picture shows a model of one kind of object that is too tiny to see—a methane molecule. Scientists use models of molecules to explain why atoms act as they do and to predict how substances will react chemically with each other.

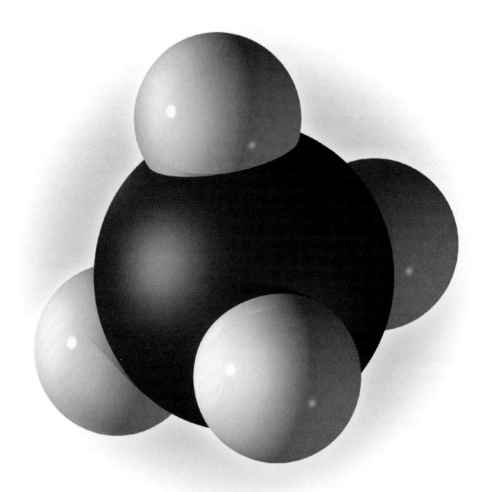

Methane Molecule

Practice Making and Using Models

Materials

- 2 different colors of clay
- toothpicks, broken in half

Follow This Procedure

1. Make a chart like the one shown. Use your chart to draw your molecules.

2. You will make clay models of molecules that contain hydrogen and oxygen atoms. Use one color of clay to make oxygen atoms for your model molecules. Use another color for hydrogen atoms.

3. Use the clay "atoms" to construct molecules of water, hydrogen peroxide, and hydrogen gas. The table shows how many atoms to include in each molecule and how the atoms are connected.

4. Complete the chart by making a drawing of your model.

Thinking About Your Thinking

How does having a physical model help you understand these molecules? Use your models to explain how the molecules of different substances vary.

Name	Atoms in one molecule	Arrangement	Drawing of molecule model
Water	2 hydrogen 1 oxygen	H\O/H	
Hydrogen peroxide	2 hydrogen 2 oxygen	H—O—O—H	
Hydrogen gas	2 hydrogen	H—H	

Formulating Questions and Hypotheses

Asking questions is an important part of the scientific process. Questions may come from a problem you have, from something you observe, or from things that interest you.

After you've identified a question, the next step is to formulate a hypothesis. Your hypothesis should be a clear statement that answers your question. A good hypothesis should also be testable. You should be able to design an experiment that would prove that your hypothesis is true or false.

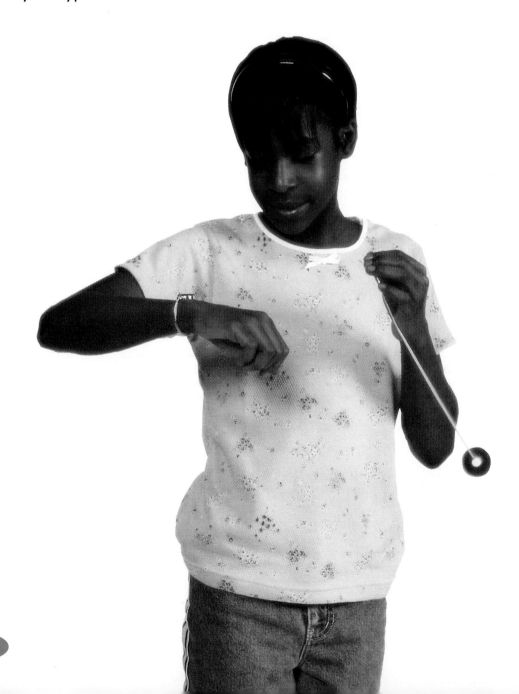

Practice Formulating Questions and Hypotheses

Materials

- scissors
- metric ruler
- string
- metal washer
- clock with a second hand

Follow This Procedure:

1. Make a chart like the one shown. Use your chart to record your data.

2. Cut and measure the length of a piece of string. Your string should be between 25 cm and 45 cm long. Record the length in your chart.

3. Tie a washer to one end of the string to make a pendulum.

4. Hold the washer out at about a 45° angle. This position is the start point for timing the period of the pendulum.

5. Release the washer. When the washer has swung back to the start point, one period has passed. Time how long it takes for 5 periods of the pendulum to occur. Record the time in your chart.

6. How do you think the length of the string affects the time it takes for one period? Write a hypothesis.

7. Test your hypothesis. Repeat steps 3–5 four more times, using a different length of string each time.

String length	Time for one period

Thinking About Your Thinking

On what information did you base your hypothesis? Did your data support your hypothesis? What other questions do you have as a result of this activity?

Collecting and Interpreting Data

How can you organize and interpret information that you collect?

When you make observations, you collect and interpret data. Arranging your data in graphs, tables, charts, or diagrams can make it easier to solve problems or answer questions. The best method of arranging your data depends on the type of data you collect and the way you plan to use it.

The graphics below display the same data in two different ways. Which graphic would you use to compare the growth of the two plants?

Plant Growth					
	Day 1	Day 2	Day 3	Day 4	Day 5
Plant in soil	3.0 cm	4.0 cm	4.5 cm	5.3 cm	6.0 cm
Plant in sand	3.0 cm	3.2 cm	3.6 cm	4.0 cm	4.1 cm

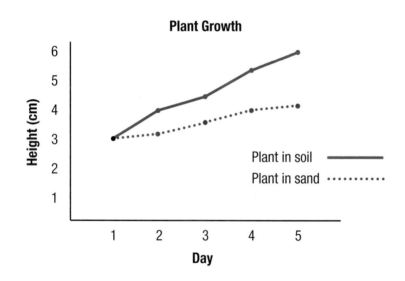

Practice Collecting and Interpreting Data

Follow This Procedure:

1. Work with a group. Collect the following data from each group member:

   - How many people are in the person's family?
   - What is the person's height?
   - What color is the person's hair?
   - What is the person's eye color
   - How many years has the person lived in your city?

2. Decide with your group how to organize and display the data.

3. Discuss with your group how you would interpret these data. What might these data help you say about your group as a whole?

Thinking About Your Thinking

Why did you organize the data in the manner you chose? Could you present it in another way to emphasize a different view of your group? What other information would you add to your data to give a better picture of your group?

25

Identifying and Controlling Variables

How can you identify and control variables?

A variable is any factor that can change the outcome of an experiment. When you do experiments, it is important to identify and control variables. You do this by finding out which conditions make a difference in an experiment. To find how a particular variable affects the outcome of an experiment, you must control all other variables.

For example, suppose you wanted to find out whether more sugar dissolves in cold water or warm water. What variables would you control? What variable would change?

Practice Identifying and Controlling Variables

Materials

- measuring cup
- cold water
- 2 plastic cups
- 2 plastic spoons
- sugar
- very warm water

Follow This Procedure

1 Place 250 mL of cold water into a plastic cup.

2 Slowly add a half spoonful of sugar. Stir until all the sugar dissolves.

3 Keep adding sugar until no more will dissolve. Stir after each addition. Record the total amount of sugar you added to the cold water.

4 How much sugar will dissolve in very warm water? Decide how to test the warm water so that you can accurately compare it to the cold water. Decide on the following with your group as you develop a procedure to test the warm water.

- How much water should you use?

- How much sugar should you add at one time?

- Should you stir or not stir? If you stir, how long should you stir?

5 Use your procedure to test the warm water. Compare your results to those from the cold water.

Thinking About Your Thinking

How much warm water did you use? Why did you choose that amount? What variables did you control? Why?

Experimenting

How can you perform valuable experiments?

Scientific experiments test a hypothesis or attempt to solve a problem. The results of the investigation can be used to form a conclusion about the hypothesis or to state an answer to the problem.

First, state the problem you are investigating as a clear question and write a hypothesis. Then identify the variables that might affect the results of your investigation. Identify the variable you will change. Keep all other variables the same.

Next, design your experiment. Write down the steps that you will use.

When you do the experiment, record your data clearly so that other people can understand what you did and how you did it. Your results should always be reported honestly, even if they were different from what you expected.

Finally, interpret your data and state your conclusions.

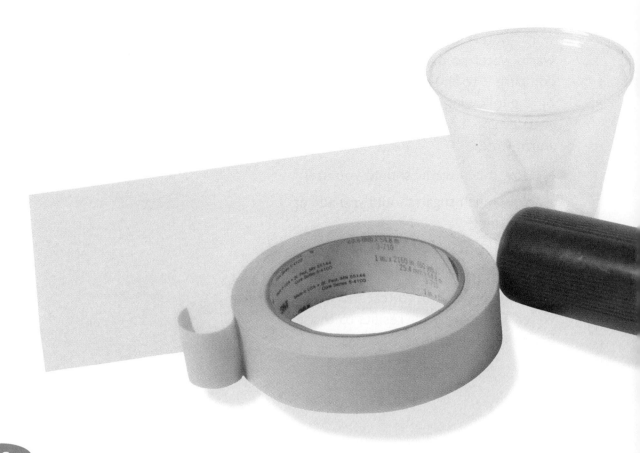

Practice Experimenting

Materials

- tape
- cup
- flashlight
- metric ruler

Follow This Procedure

1 Think about what you know about shadows. How does the distance between an object and a source of light affect the size of the object's shadow?

2 On a sheet of paper write a hypothesis to answer this question.

3 Design an experiment to test your hypotheses. Write a procedure. Use the materials in the materials list to do your experiment. Remember to identify and control the variables.

4 Make a chart to record your data.

5 Perform your experiment, following the steps in your procedure. Be sure to record your data.

6 Interpret your data and state your conclusion.

Thinking About Your Thinking

What is the difference between a hypothesis, as in step 2, and a conclusion, as in step 6? What information is your hypothesis based on? What information is your conclusion based on?

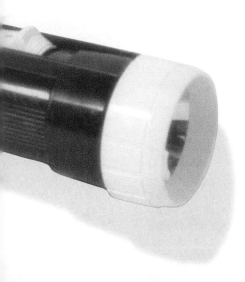

Classification of Living Things

Scientists classify different species of organisms into the five kingdoms you see below. All organisms that are now living or once lived can be placed into one of these kingdoms. Organisms within each kingdom share certain traits. Grouping organisms in this manner helps scientists learn more about them.

Kingdom	Monera	Protist	Fungi	Plant	Animal
Type of Cells	Prokaryotic	Eukaryotic	Eukaryotic	Eukaryotic	Eukaryotic
One-celled or Many-celled	One-celled	One-and many-celled	One-and many-celled	One-and many-celled	Many-celled
Movement	Some move	Some move	None move	None move	All move
Nutrition	Some make their own food. Others get it from other organisms.	Some make their own food. Others get it from other organisms.	All get food from other organisms.	All make their own food.	Eat plants or other animals.

▲ Protist

◀ Fungi

Animal ▼

Monera ▼

Plant ▶

Circuits

Electric current can flow only when it can follow a complete circuit. In series circuits, the current has only one path it can follow. Current can travel in more than one path in a parallel circuit.

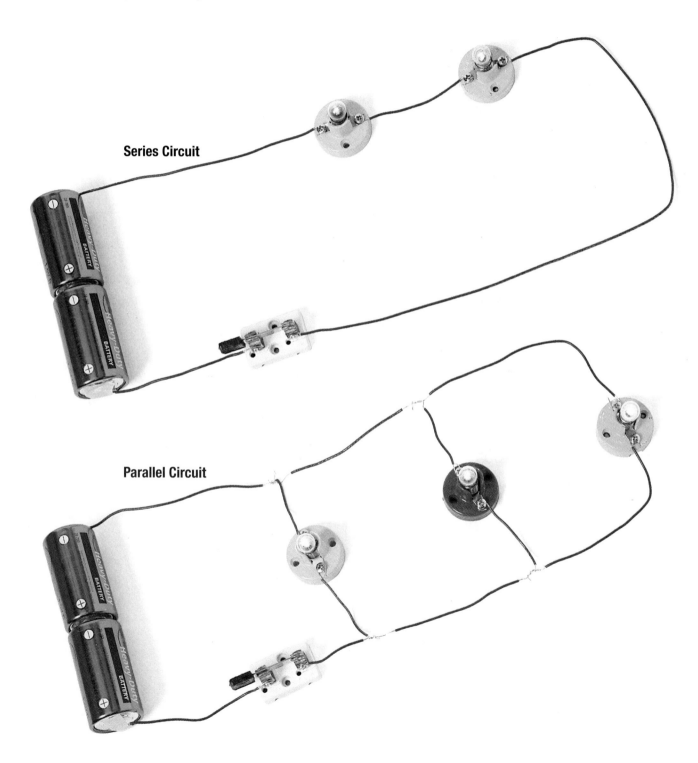

Series Circuit

Parallel Circuit

Energy in our World

The sun is the source of all energy on the earth. In fact, electromagnetic radiation of about 100 thousand million million joules reaches the earth from the sun each second. This energy is converted to different forms. You can follow some of these energy conversions in the pictures below.

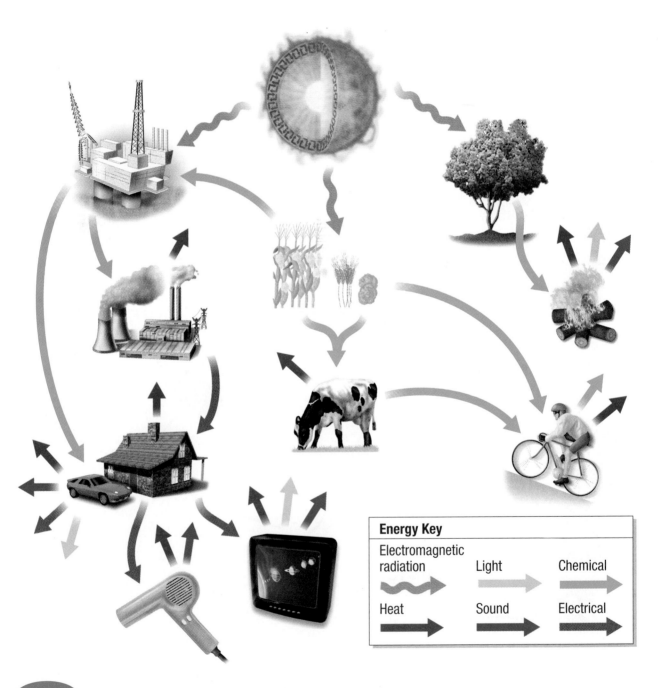

Energy Key

Electromagnetic radiation	Light	Chemical
Heat	Sound	Electrical

Simple Machines

Machines make work easier. Machines can be very simple, like the four simple machines shown on this page, or they can be complicated machines, such as automobiles.

Lever

Pulley

Wheel and Axle

Inclined Plane

Rock Cycle

Scientists classify rocks into three main types—igneous, metamorphic, and sedimentary. Each type of rock forms at least partly from other rocks. All rocks undergo continuous changes, which are brought about by heat, pressure, chemical reactions, or other forces that wear away or deposit materials. This change of rock from one type to another in a sequence is called the rock cycle.

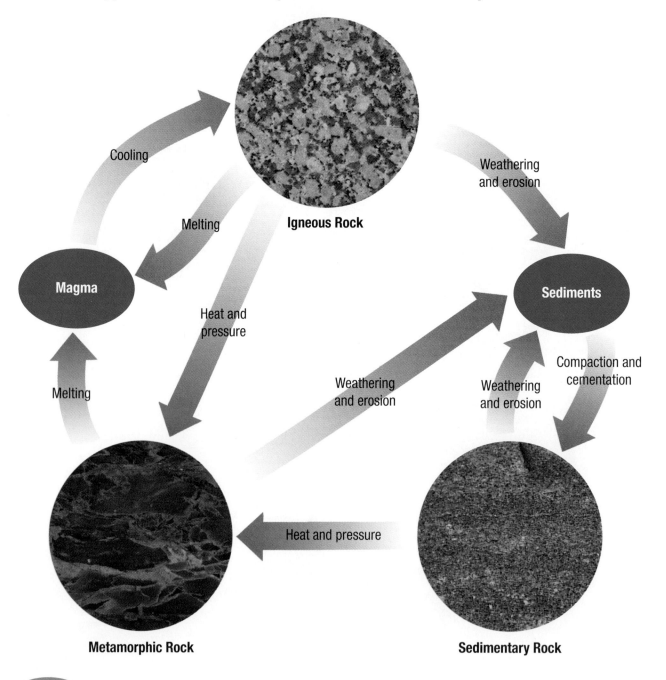

Cooling

Melting

Igneous Rock

Weathering and erosion

Magma

Heat and pressure

Sediments

Melting

Weathering and erosion

Weathering and erosion

Compaction and cementation

Heat and pressure

Metamorphic Rock

Sedimentary Rock

Characteristics of Planets

Planet	Mercury	Venus	Earth	Mars	Jupiter	Saturn	Uranus	Neptune	Pluto
Average distance to sun (AU)	0.387	0.723	1.000	1.524	5.203	9.529	19.191	30.061	39.529
Period of rotation days hours minutes	58 15 28	243 00 14	00 23 56	00 24 37	00 09 55	00 10 39	00 17 14	00 16 03	06 09 17
Period of revolution	87.97 days	224.70 days	365.26 days	686.98 days	11.86 years	29.46 years	84.04 years	164.79 years	248.53 years
Diameter	4,878	12,104	12,756	6,794	142,796	120,660	51,118	49,528	2,290
Mass (Earth=1)	0.06	0.82	1.00	0.11	317.83	95.15	14.54	17.23	0.002
Density (g/cm³)	5.42	5.24	5.50	3.94	1.31	0.70	1.30	1.66	2.03
Surface gravity (Earth=1)	0.38	0.90	1.00	0.38	2.53	1.07	0.92	1.12	0.06
Number of known satellites	0	0	1	2	16	18	15	8	1
Known rings	0	0	0	0	4	thousands	11	4	0

Layers of the Atmosphere

Earth's atmosphere extends thousands of kilometers above Earth's surface. The higher you go, the thinner the atmosphere becomes. You can see the four layers of the atmosphere below. The ionosphere is an area of the atmosphere that is made up of ions that reflect radio waves.

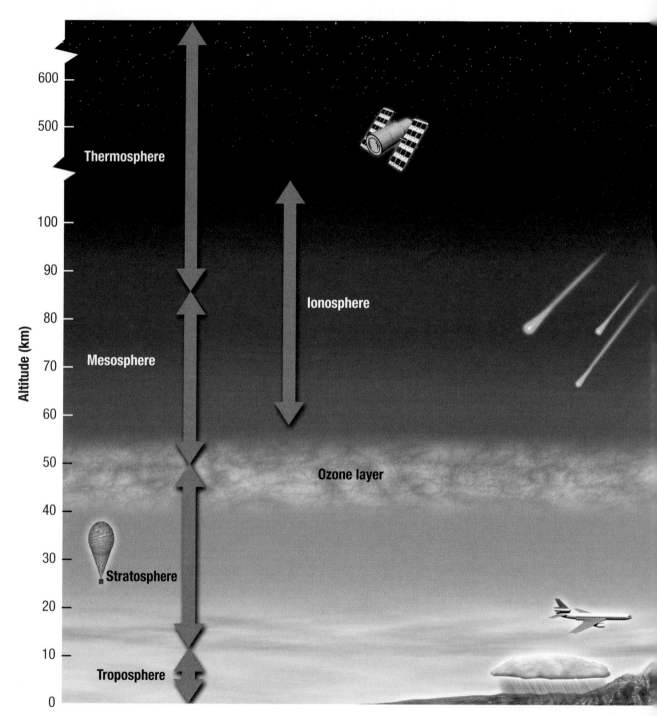

Atoms and Molecules

All matter is made of atoms, which are made of protons, neutrons, and electrons. Neutrons and protons form the nucleus of the atom. Electrons constantly change their positions as they travel around the nucleus. Atoms chemically combine to form a molecule.

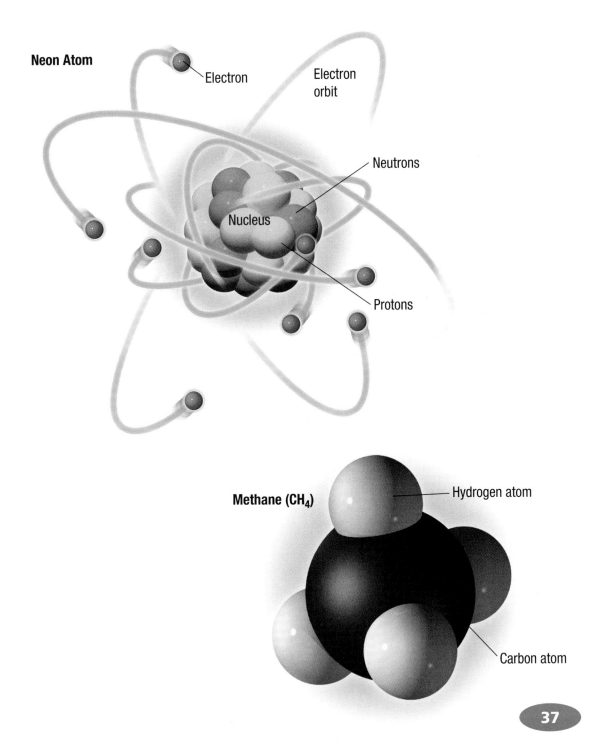

Neon Atom

Electron

Electron orbit

Neutrons

Nucleus

Protons

Methane (CH_4)

Hydrogen atom

Carbon atom

The Human Body

The different organs in your body make up organ systems. The parts of a simple system work together to perform a function. In a similar way, the organs in a system in your body work together to perform a function. All the systems work together to make your body work.

Respiratory System

◀ *Your respiratory system helps bring oxygen to the cells of your body and carries carbon dioxide and other wastes from cells. Air you breathe enters your lungs and passes into blood vessels that take it to all your cells.*

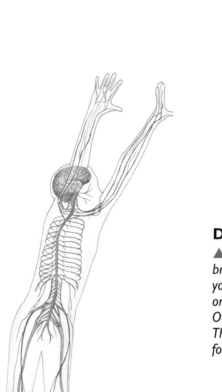

Digestive System

▲ *Organs in your digestive system break down food into nutrients that your cells can use. Some of the organs grind and mash the food. Others produce digestive fluids. Then blood vessels carry digested foods to all the cells of your body.*

Nervous System

◀ *Your nervous system includes your brain, spinal cord, and nerves. It gathers information from your environment, passes information to different parts of your body, and helps you interpret and use the information. Your brain sends signals to your muscles to let you move. Nerves send messages to and from other organs so they function properly.*

Circulatory System

Your heart, blood, and blood vessels make up your circulatory system. This system carries nutrients from your digestive system, oxygen brought in by your respiratory system, and wastes from both systems. These substances are transported to and from your body cells. ▶

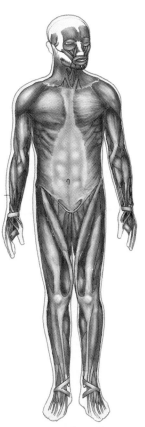

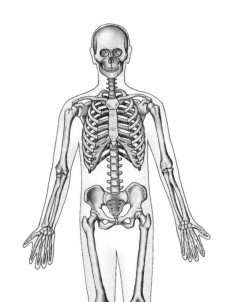

Muscular System

▲ *Many of the muscles in your body make up the muscular system. These muscles work with your bones to move the parts of your body. Nerves control the muscles. Blood vessels bring them the nutrients and oxygen they need to work.*

Skeletal System

◀ *All the bones in your body make up the skeletal system. They work together to protect and support your body and to help it move.*

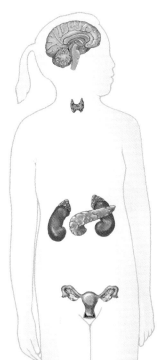

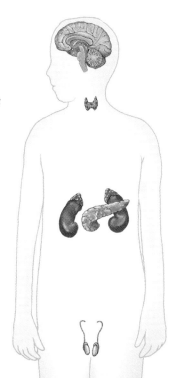

Endocrine System

◀ *The endocrine system is made up of glands that secrete hormones directly into the blood. These hormones control certain functions in your body.* ▶

Tools of Science

Scientists use a variety of tools. You too will use tools as you do science activities. Some of those tools are shown on these two pages.

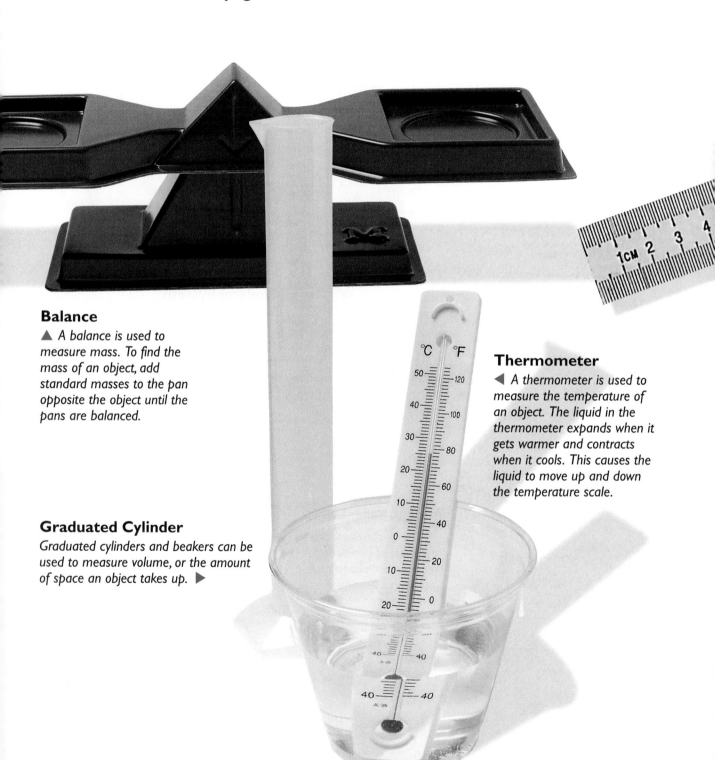

Balance
▲ *A balance is used to measure mass. To find the mass of an object, add standard masses to the pan opposite the object until the pans are balanced.*

Graduated Cylinder
Graduated cylinders and beakers can be used to measure volume, or the amount of space an object takes up. ▶

Thermometer
◀ *A thermometer is used to measure the temperature of an object. The liquid in the thermometer expands when it gets warmer and contracts when it cools. This causes the liquid to move up and down the temperature scale.*

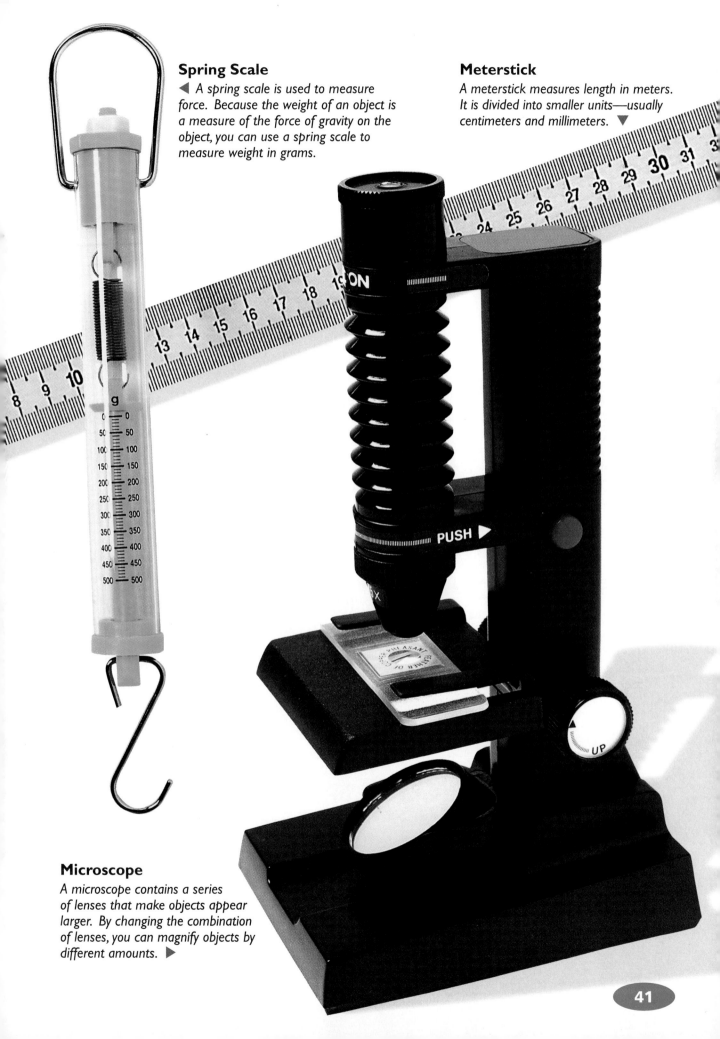

Spring Scale

◀ *A spring scale is used to measure force. Because the weight of an object is a measure of the force of gravity on the object, you can use a spring scale to measure weight in grams.*

Meterstick

A meterstick measures length in meters. It is divided into smaller units—usually centimeters and millimeters. ▼

Microscope

A microscope contains a series of lenses that make objects appear larger. By changing the combination of lenses, you can magnify objects by different amounts. ▶

41

Periodic Table
of the Elements

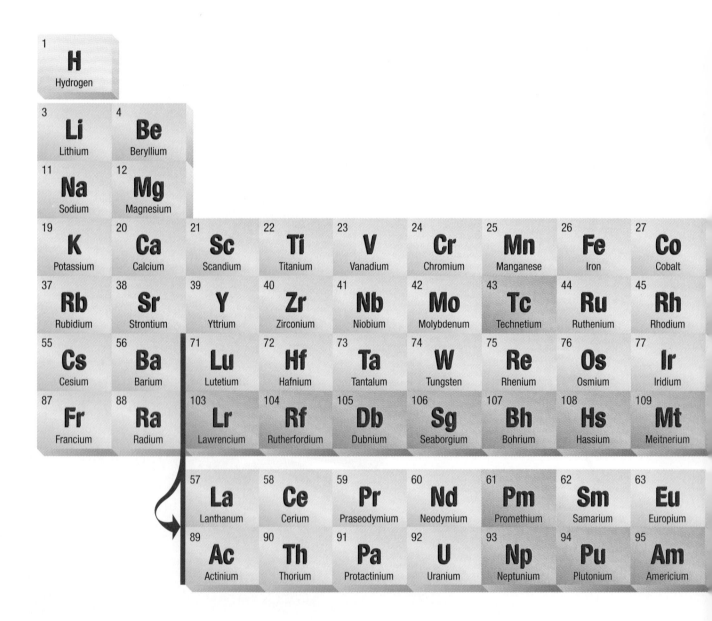

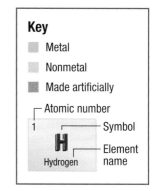

Key

- ▨ Metal
- ▨ Nonmetal
- ▨ Made artificially

Atomic number

Symbol

Element name

1		
H		
Hydrogen		

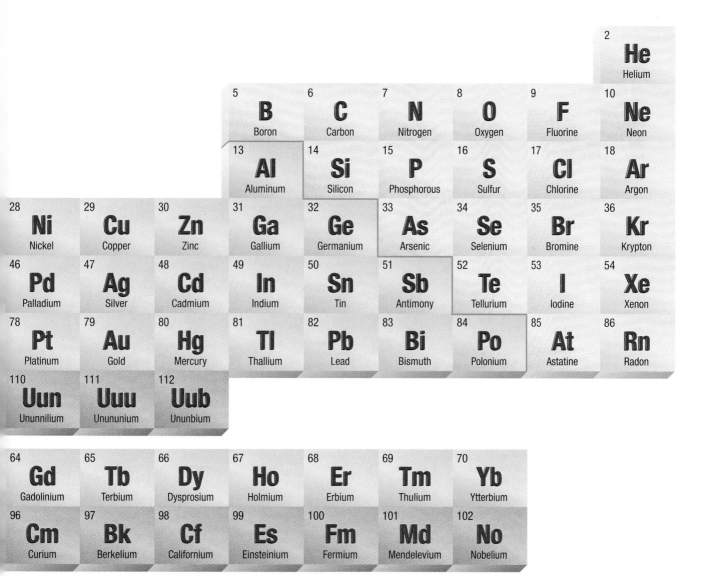

																2
																He Helium

5 **B** Boron	6 **C** Carbon	7 **N** Nitrogen	8 **O** Oxygen	9 **F** Fluorine	10 **Ne** Neon
13 **Al** Aluminum	14 **Si** Silicon	15 **P** Phosphorous	16 **S** Sulfur	17 **Cl** Chlorine	18 **Ar** Argon

28 **Ni** Nickel	29 **Cu** Copper	30 **Zn** Zinc	31 **Ga** Gallium	32 **Ge** Germanium	33 **As** Arsenic	34 **Se** Selenium	35 **Br** Bromine	36 **Kr** Krypton
46 **Pd** Palladium	47 **Ag** Silver	48 **Cd** Cadmium	49 **In** Indium	50 **Sn** Tin	51 **Sb** Antimony	52 **Te** Tellurium	53 **I** Iodine	54 **Xe** Xenon
78 **Pt** Platinum	79 **Au** Gold	80 **Hg** Mercury	81 **Tl** Thallium	82 **Pb** Lead	83 **Bi** Bismuth	84 **Po** Polonium	85 **At** Astatine	86 **Rn** Radon
110 **Uun** Ununnilium	111 **Uuu** Unununium	112 **Uub** Ununbium						

64 **Gd** Gadolinium	65 **Tb** Terbium	66 **Dy** Dysprosium	67 **Ho** Holmium	68 **Er** Erbium	69 **Tm** Thulium	70 **Yb** Ytterbium
96 **Cm** Curium	97 **Bk** Berkelium	98 **Cf** Californium	99 **Es** Einsteinium	100 **Fm** Fermium	101 **Md** Mendelevium	102 **No** Nobelium

History of Science

8000 B.C.	6000 B.C.	4000 B.C	2000 B.C.

Life Science

Physical Science

● **3000 B.C.**
The Egyptians develop geometry. They use it to re-measure their farmlands after floods of the Nile River.

Earth Science

● **8000 B.C.** Farming communities start as people use the plow for farming.

Human Body

44

4th century B.C.
Aristotle classifies
plants and animals.

3rd century B.C.
Aristarchus proposes that the
earth revolves around the sun.

4th century B.C.
Aristotle describes the
motions of falling
bodies. He believes that
heavier things fall faster
than lighter things.

260 B.C. Archimedes
discovers the principles of
buoyancy and the lever.

4th century B.C. Aristotle
describes the motions
of the planets.

200 B.C. Eratosthenes calculates
the size of the earth. His result is
very close to the earth's actual
size.

87 B.C.
Chinese report observing
an object in the sky that
later became known as
Halley's comet.

5th and 4th centuries B.C.
Hippocrates and other Greek
doctors record the symptoms of
many diseases. They also urge
people to eat a well-balanced diet.

**Life
Science**

**Physical
Science**

83 A.D.
Chinese travelers
use the compass
for navigation.

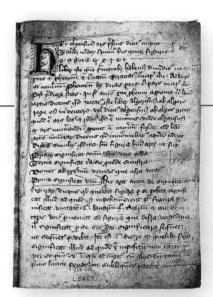

**About
750–1250**
Islamic scholars get
scientific books
from Europe. They
translate them into
Arabic and add
more information.

**Earth
Science**

140 Claudius Ptolemy
draws a complete picture of
an earth-centered universe.

132 The Chinese make the
first seismograph, a device
that measures the strength
of earthquakes.

**Human
Body**

2nd century Galen
writes about anatomy
and the causes of
diseases.

1100s
Animal guide books begin to appear. They describe what animals look like and give facts about them.

1250
Albert the Great describes plants and animals in his book *On Vegetables and On Animals.*

1555
Pierre Belon finds similarities between the skeletons of humans and birds.

9th century
The Chinese invent block printing. By the 11th century, they had movable type.

1019
Abu Arrayhan Muhammad ibn Ahmad al'Biruni observed both a solar and lunar eclipse within a few months of each other.

1543
Nikolaus Copernicus publishes his book *On The Revolutions of the Celestial Orbs.* It says that the sun remains still and the earth moves in a circle around it.

1265
Nasir al-Din al-Tusi gets his own observatory. His ideas about how the planets move will influence Nikolaus Copernicus.

About 1000
Ibn Sina writes an encyclopedia of medical knowledge. For many years, doctors will use this as their main source of medical knowledge. Arab scientist Ibn Al-Haytham gives the first detailed explanation of how we see and how light forms images in our eyes.

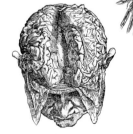

1543
Andreas Vesalius publishes *On the Makeup of the Human Body.* In this book he gives very detailed pictures of human anatomy.

1600	1620	1640	1660	1680

Life Science

1663 Robert Hooke first sees the cells of living organisms through a microscope. Antoni van Leeuwenhoek discovers bacteria with the microscope in 1674.

1679 Maria Sibylla Merian paints the first detailed pictures of a caterpillar turning into a butterfly. She also develops new techniques for printing pictures.

Physical Science

1600 William Gilbert describes the behavior of magnets. He also shows that the attraction of a compass needle toward North is due to the earth's magnetic pole.

1632 Galileo Galilei shows that all objects fall at the same speed. Galileo also shows that all matter has inertia.

1687 Isaac Newton introduces his three laws of motion.

Earth Science

1609–1619 Johannes Kepler introduces the three laws of planetary motion.

1610 Galileo uses a telescope to see the rings around the planet Saturn and the moons of Jupiter.

1669 Nicolaus Steno sets forth the basic principles of how to date rock layers.

1650 Maria Cunitz publishes a new set of tables to help astronomers find the positions of the planets and stars.

1693–1698 Maria Eimmart draws 250 pictures depicting the phases of the moon. She also paints flowers and insects.

1687 Isaac Newton introduces the concept of gravity.

Human Body

1628 William Harvey shows how the heart circulates blood through the blood vessels.

48

1735 Carolus Linnaeus devises the modern system of naming living things.

1759 Emile du Châtelet translates Isaac Newton's work into French. Her work still remains the only French translation.

1789 Antoine-Laurent Lavoisier claims that certain substances, such as oxygen, hydrogen, and nitrogen, cannot be broken down into anything simpler. He calls these substances "elements."

1704 Isaac Newton publishes his views on optics. He shows that white light contains many colors.

1729 Stephen Gray shows that electricity flows in a straight path from one place to another.

1781 Caroline and William Herschel (sister and brother) discover the planet Uranus.

1784 French chemist Antoine-Laurent Lavoisier does the first extensive study of respiration.

1798 Edward Jenner reports the first successful vaccination for smallpox.

1721 Onesimus introduces to America the African method for inoculation against smallpox.

1805	1810	1815	1820	1825	1830	1835

Life Science

1808 French naturalist Georges Cuvier describes some fossilized bones as belonging to a giant, extinct marine lizard.

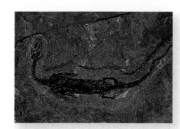

1838–1839 Matthias Schleiden and Theodor Schwann describe the cell as the basic unit of a living organism.

Physical Science

1800 Alessandro Volta makes the first dry cell (battery).

1820 H.C. Oersted discovers that a wire with electric current running through it will deflect a compass needle. This showed that electricity and magnetism were related.

1808 John Dalton proposes that all matter is made of atoms.

Earth Science

1830 Charles Lyell writes *Principles of Geology*. This is the first modern geology textbook.

1803 Luke Howard assigns to clouds the basic names that we still use today— cumulus, stratus, and cirrus.

Human Body

1842 Richard Owen gives the name "dinosaurs" to the extinct giant lizards.

1859 Charles Darwin proposes the theory of evolution by natural selection.

1863 Gregor Mendel shows that certain traits in peas are passed to succeeding generations in a regular fashion. He outlines the methods of heredity.

1847 Hermann Helmholtz states the law of conservation of energy. This law holds that energy cannot be created or destroyed. Energy only can be changed from one form to another.

1842 Christian Doppler explains why a car, train, plane, or any quickly moving object sounds higher pitched as it approaches and lower pitched as it moves away.

1866 Ernst Haeckel proposes the term "ecology" for the study of the environment.

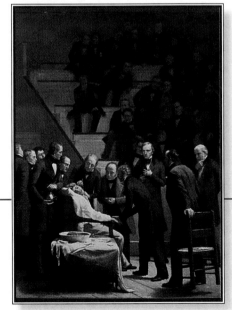

Early 1860s Louis Pasteur realizes that tiny organisms cause wine and milk to turn sour. He shows that heating the liquids kills these germs. This process is called pasteurization.

1840s Doctors use anesthetic drugs to put their patients to sleep.

1850s and 1860s Ignaz P. Semmelweis and Sir Joseph Lister pioneer the use of antiseptics in medicine.

Life Science

● **1900–1910** George Washington Carver, the son of slave parents, develops many new uses for old crops. He finds a way to make soybeans into rubber, cotton into road-paving material, and peanuts into paper.

Physical Science

● **1897** J. J. Thomson discovers the electron.

1895 Wilhelm Roentgen discovers X rays. ●

1896 Henri Becquerel discovers radioactivity. ●

● **1905** Albert Einstein introduces the theory of relativity.

Earth Science

1907 ● Bertram Boltwood introduces the idea of "radioactive" dating. This allows geologists to accurately measure the age of a fossil.

1912 ● Alfred Wegener proposes the theory of continental drift. This theory says that all land on the earth was once a single mass. It eventually broke apart and the continents slowly drifted away from each other.

Human Body

● **1885** Louis Pasteur gives the first vaccination for rabies. Pasteur thought that tiny organisms caused most diseases.

● **1920s** Ernest Everett Just performs important research into how cells metabolize food.

● **1947** Archaeologist Mary Leakey unearths the skull of a *Proconsul africanus,* an example of a fossilized ape.

● **1913** Danish physicist Niels Bohr presents the modern theory of the atom.

● **1911** Ernst Rutherford discovers that atoms have a nucleus, or center.

● **1911** Marie Curie wins the Nobel Prize for chemistry. This makes her the first person ever to win two Nobel Prizes, the highest award a scientist can receive.

● **1938** Otto Hahn and Fritz Straussman split the uranium atom. This marks the beginning of the nuclear age.

● **1942** Enrico Fermi and Leo Szilard produce the first nuclear chain reaction.

● **1945** The first atomic bomb is exploded in the desert at Alamogordo, New Mexico.

● **1938** Lise Meitner and Otto Frisch explain how an atom can split in two.

● **1946** Vincent Schaefer and Irving Langmuir use dry ice to produce the first artificial rain.

1933 ●
Meteorologist Tor Bergeron explains how raindrops form in clouds.

● **1917** Florence Sabin becomes the first woman professor at an American medical college.

● **1928** Alexander Fleming notices that the molds in his petri dish produced a substance, later called an antibiotic, that killed bacteria. He calls this substance penicillin.

● **1935** Chemist Percy Julian develops physostigmine, a drug used to fight the eye disease glaucoma.

● **1922** Doctors inject the first diabetes patient with insulin.

1950	1955	1960	1965	1970

Life Science

1951 Barbara McClintock discovers that genes can move to different places on a chromosome.

1953 The collective work of James D. Watson, Francis Crick, Maurice Wilkins, and Rosalind Franklin leads to the discovery of the structure of the DNA molecule.

1972 Researchers find human DNA to be 99% similar to that of chimpanzees.

Physical Science

1969 UCLA is host to the first computer node of ARPANET, the forerunner of the internet.

1974 Opening of TRIUMF, the world's largest particle accelerator, at the University of British Columbia.

Earth Science

1957 The first human-made object goes into orbit when the Soviet Union launches *Sputnik I*.

1969 Neil Armstrong is the first person to walk on the moon.

1972 Cygnus X-1 is first identified as a blackhole.

1967 Geophysicists introduce the theory of plate tectonics.

1962 John Glenn is the first American to orbit the earth.

Human Body

1954–1962 In 1954, Jonas Salk introduced the first vaccine for polio. In 1962, most doctors and hospitals substituted Albert Sabin's orally administered vaccine.

1967 Dr. Christiaan Barnard performs the first successful human heart transplant operation.

1964 The surgeon general's report on the hazards of smoking is released.

1988
Congress approves funding for the Human Genome Project. This project will map and sequence the human genetic code.

1997
Scientists in Edinburgh, Scotland, successfully clone a sheep, Dolly.

1975 The first personal computer goes for sale: The Altair.

1996 Scientists make "element 112" in the laboratory. This is the heaviest element yet created.

1979 A near meltdown occurs at the Three Mile Island nuclear power plant in Pennsylvania. This alerts the nation to the dangers of nuclear power.

1995 The first "extra-solar" planet is discovered.

Early 1990s The National Severe Storms Laboratory develops NEXRAD, the national network of Doppler weather radar stations for early severe storm warnings.

1976 National Academy of Sciences reports on the dangers of chlorofluorocarbons (CFCs) for the earth's ozone layer.

1981 The first commercial Magnetic Resonance Imaging scanners are available. Doctors use MRI scanners to look at the non-bony parts of the body.

1982 Dr. Stanley Prusiner identifies a new kind of disease-causing agent—prions. Prions are responsible for many brain disorders.

1998 John Glenn, age 77, orbits the earth aboard the space shuttle *Discovery*. Glenn is the oldest person to fly in space.

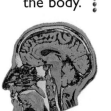

Glossary

A

acceleration (ak sel′ə rā′shən), the change in velocity during a particular time period.

acid (a′sid), a compound that releases hydrogen ions in water.

adaptation (ad′ap tā′shən), an inherited trait that helps a species survive in its environment.

addiction (ə dik′shən), a disease affecting both the mind and body that makes people unable to go without something, such as a drug.

air mass (er mas), a large body of air having similar properties or weather conditions.

air pressure (er presh′ər), the force of air against Earth's surface.

air resistance (er ri zis′təns), the friction from air molecules hitting an object as the object moves through the air.

alcohol (al′kə hȯl), depressant drug found in beer, wine, and liquor.

alcoholic (al′kə hȯ lik), a person who does not have control over his or her drinking.

alcoholism (al′kə hȯ liz′əm), a disease in which a person is unable to stop abusing alcohol.

alternative energy sources (ȯl tėr′nə tiv en ər jē sȯrs), source of energy other than fossil fuels.

amplitude (am′plə tüd), the distance between a wave's midpoint and its crest or trough.

anemometer (an′ə mom′ə tər), an instrument used to measure wind speed.

aquifer (ak′wə fər), a layer of rock in which ground water can accumulate and flow freely.

asexual reproduction (ā sek′shü əl rē prə duk′shən), reproduction by one parent.

auroras (ô ror′əz), the glow or display of lights in the skies near polar latitudes.

axon (ak′son), part of a neuron that carries messages away from the cell body.

B

balanced forces (bal′enst fôrs′əs), equal forces acting in opposite directions.

barometer (bə rom′ə tər), an instrument used to measure air pressure.

base (bās), a compound that releases hydroxide ions when dissolved in water.

base (bās), one kind of molecule that makes up a DNA strand.

behavioral adaptation (bi hā′vyər əl ad′ap tā′shən), an action that aids survival.

big bang theory (big bang thē′ar ē), the idea that the universe started with a huge explosion about 15 billion years ago.

biome (bī′ōm), large geographic region with a particular kind of climate and community.

black hole (blak hōl), an invisible object in space whose mass and gravitational force is so great that not even light can escape.

brain stem (brān stem), part of the brain that controls involuntary actions, such as breathing; connects the brain to the spinal cord.

C

caffeine (kaf′ēn), a mild stimulant found in coffee, tea, colas, and chocolate.

carbon monoxide (kär′bən mo nok′sīd), a gas found in cigarette smoke that replaces some of the blood's oxygen when inhaled.

carnivore (kär′nə vôr), a consumer that eats only animals.

cell division (sel də vizh′ən), the dividing of a cell following mitosis.

cell membrane (sel mem′brān), thin outer covering that holds a cell together.

cell theory (sel thē′ər ē), theory stating that the cell is the basic unit of all living organisms, and only living cells can produce new living cells.

cell wall (sel wôl), tough, nonliving material that acts like an outside skeleton for each plant cell.

central nervous system (sen′trəl nėr′vəs sis′təm), part of the nervous system made up of the brain and spinal cord.

cerebellum (ser′ə bel′əm), part of the brain that coordinates movements and helps maintain balance.

cerebrum (sə rē′brəm), part of the brain that controls thinking and voluntary movements and receives information from the senses.

chemical equation (kem′ə kel i kwā′zhən), an arrangement of symbols and formulas used to show what happens during a chemical reaction.

chlorophyll (klôr′ə fil), green substance in chloroplasts that traps energy from sunlight.

chloroplast (klôr′ə plast), organelle that makes sugars, using carbon dioxide, water, and the energy from sunlight.

chromosome (kro′mə sōm), stringlike structure in a cell nucleus that carries information controlling all the cell's activities.

competition (kom′pə tish′ən), a situation in which two or more organisms attempt to use the same resource.

compound microscope (kom′pound mī′krə skōp), microscope having more than one lens.

compressional wave (kəm presh′ən əl wāv), wave in which matter vibrates in the same direction as the energy waves traveling through it.

concave mirror (kon kāv′ mir′ər), a mirror whose center curves away from an object.

concentrated (kon′sən trā′tid), describes a solution with a large amount of solute compared to the amount of solvent.

condensation (kon′den sā′shən), the change of state from a gas to a liquid.

conservation (kon′sər vā′shən), careful use of resources so they will last longer.

convex mirror (con veks′ mir′ər), a mirror whose center curves toward an object.

corona (kə rō′nə), a crown of glowing gases around the sun that can be seen during a total solar eclipse.

cytoplasm (sī′tə plaz′əm), clear, jellylike material that fills the space between the cell membrane and the nucleus.

D

dendrite (den′drīt), part of a neuron that collects information from other neurons.

depressant (di pres′nt), a drug that slows down the nervous system.

dew point (dü point), the temperature at which a volume of air cannot hold any more water vapor.

dilute (dī lüt′), describes a solution with a small amount of solute compared to the amount of solvent.

displacement (dis plās′mənt), the direction and shortest distance traveled during a change of position.

distance (dis′təns), the total length of the path between two points.

DNA (dē en ā), the molecule in each cell that directs the cell's activities.

dominant gene (dom′ə nənt jēn), a gene that prevents the expression of another gene.

Doppler radar (dop′lər rā′där), a type of radar that calculates distance and shows direction of movement.

drainage basin (drā′nij bā sin), the land area from which a river system gets its water.

drug (drug), a substance that acts on the body to change the way it works.

drug abuse (drug ə byüz), using drugs for purposes other than health.

E

endocrine gland (en′dō krən gland), a tissue or organ that releases chemical substances into the bloodstream.

endocrine system (en′dō krən sis′təm), body system consisting of glands, hormones, and target cells that work together to control various functions in the body.

endoplasmic reticulum (en′dō plaz′mik ri tik′yə ləm), organelle that transports materials inside the cell.

endothermic reaction (en′dō thėr′mik rē ak′shən), a chemical reaction in which more energy is taken in than given off.

energy pyramid (en′ər Jē pir′ə mid), a model that shows how energy is used in a food chain or an ecosystem.

equinox (ē′kwə noks), a point in the Earth's orbit around the sun where nights and days are the same length.

estuary (es′chü er′ē), place where fresh water from rivers or streams mixes with saltwater from the ocean.

evaporation (i vap′ə rā′shən), the change of a state from liquid to gas at the surface of a liquid.

evolution (ev′ə lü shən), process that results in changes in the genetic makeup of a species over very long periods of time.

exothermic reaction (ek′sō thėr′mik rē ak′shən), a chemical reaction in which more energy is given off than is taken in.

F

fault (fôlt), a crack in the earth's crust along which rock moves.

fertilization (fėr′tl ə zā′shən), the joining of an egg cell and a sperm cell during sexual reproduction.

focal point (fō′kəl point), the point at which light rays meet when reflected or refracted.

focus (fō′kəs), the point along a fault where rock first breaks or moves, causing an earthquake.

force (fôrs), a push or a pull.

forecast (fôr′kast′), a prediction of what the weather will be like in the near future.

formula (fôr′myə lə), arrangement of symbols that shows both the kinds and number of atoms in a compound.

fossil fuel (fos′əl fyü′əl), fuel such as coal, natural gas, and oil that formed underground millions of years ago from decaying organic matter.

frame of reference (frām ov ref′ər əns), the object an observer uses to detect motion.

frequency (frē′kwən sē), the number or waves (crests or troughs) that pass a point in a given amount of time.

freshwater biome (fresh′wō′tər bī′ōm), water biome that has a low salt content.

friction (frik′shən), a force between surfaces that resists the movement of one surface past the other surface.

front (frunt), the boundary between warm and cold air masses.

fusion (fyü′zhen), the combining of less massive elements to form more massive elements.

G

galaxy (gal′ək sē), a system of billions of stars, gases, and dust.

gene (jēn), a section of DNA on a chromosome that controls a trait.

geologic time scale (jē ə loj′ik tīm skāl), a record of Earth's history based on events interpreted from the rock record and fossil evidence.

glacier (glā′shər), a large mass of moving ice.

gravity (grav′ə tē), the force of attraction that exists between any two objects.

groundwater (ground wô′tər), water in the ground near the Earth's surface.

H

hallucinogen (hə lü′sn ə jen), drug that affects brain activity, changing the way a person senses the world.

herbivore (hėr′bə vôr), a consumer that eats plants or other producers.

heredity (hə red′ə tē), the process by which traits are passed from parents to offspring.

hormone (hôr′mōn), chemicals released by endocrine glands that cause target cells to perform specific activities.

humidity (hyü mid′ə tē), water vapor in the air.

hurricane (hėr′ə kān), a large tropical storm that forms over warm oceans and whose winds have a velocity of at least 110 kilometers per hour.

hybrid (hī′brid), an organism with one dominant and one recessive gene for a trait.

hypothalamus (hī′pō thal′ ə məs), part of the brain that controls body temperature, hunger, thirst, and emotions.

I

index fossil (in′deks fos′əl), a fossil of an organism that existed on Earth for a short time over a large geographic area.

indicator (in′də kā′tər), a substance that changes color at a certain range of pH values.

inertia (in ėr′shə), the resistance of an object to change in its state of motion.

inhalant (in hā′lənt), drug that enters your body with the air you breathe.

inherit (in her′it), to receive from one's mother or father.

instantaneous speed (in′stən tā′nē əs spēd), the speed at any given point.

instinct (in′stingkt), an inherited behavior.

intensity (in ten′sə tē), a measure of the amount of energy in a wave.

intoxicated (in tok′sə kā′tid), experiencing the symptoms of heavy alcohol consumption.

L

laser light (lā′zer līt), light of a single wavelength with all the waves lined up.

law (lȯ), a statement that describes events or relationships that exist in nature.

lithosphere (lith′ə sfir), the solid rocky outer layer of the earth that includes the crust.

lunar eclipse (lü′nər i klips′), a darkening of the moon when it passes through Earth's shadow.

M

mass (mas), the amount of matter in an object.

meiosis (mī ō′sis), the process by which sex cells form.

meteorologist (mē′tē ə rol′ə jist), scientist who studies the weather.

mitochondria (mī′tə kon′drē ə), organelles where food and oxygen react to release energy.

mitosis (mī tō′sis), the process by which a cell produces two new identical nuclei.

moraine (mə rān′), a ridge formed when a glacier deposits its sediments.

motor neuron (mō′tər nür′on), nerve cell in the peripheral nervous system that carries information from the central nervous system to muscles and organs.

music (myü′zik), pleasant sound with regular wave patterns.

mutation (myü tā′shən), a permanent change in DNA that occurs when DNA copies itself.

N

natural selection (nach′ər əl si lek′shən), the idea that those organisms best adapted to their environment will be the ones most likely to survive and reproduce.

nebula (neb′yə lə), cloud of dust and gas in space.

nerve impulse (nėrv im′puls), message that travels from the dendrites of a neuron to the axon.

net force (net fôrs), the combination of all the forces acting on an object.

neuron (nür′on), a nerve cell.

neutralization (nü′trə li zās′shən), a process in which an acid and a base react to produce a salt and water.

newton (nüt′n), in the metric system, the unit used to measure force or weight.

nicotine (nik′ə tēn), a stimulant drug found in tobacco.

noise (noiz), sound with no regular wave patterns.

nonrenewable resource (non′ri nü′ə bəl ri sôrs′), a resource that cannot be replaced.

nucleus (nü′klē əs), part of the cell that controls activities of other cell parts.

O

octave (ok′tiv), a musical sequence in which the top note has twice the frequency of the bottom note.

omnivore (om′ni vôr), a consumer that eats both producers and consumers.

opaque (ō pāk′), does not allow light to pass through.

ore (ôr), a rock that contains enough of a mineral to be of value.

organelle (or′gə nel′), tiny structure in the cytoplasm of a cell that performs a special job.

P

peripheral nervous system (pə rif′ər əl ner′vəs sis′təm), part of the nervous system that connects the central nervous system with all other parts of the body.

permafrost (per′mə frôst′), ground that is permanently frozen.

pH scale (pē āch skāl), a set of numbers between 0 and 14 to measure the strength of acids and bases.

photon (fō′ton), a bundle of energy that is released when an atom loses some energy.

physiological adaptation (fiz′ē ə loj′ə kəl ad′ap tā′shən), adaptation that involves a body part's job of controlling a life process.

plankton (plangk′tən), microscopic, free-floating organisms that serve as food for larger organisms.

plate tectonics (plāt tek ton′iks), theory that states that the lithosphere is broken into plates that move.

pollutant (pə lüt′nt), harmful substance in the environment.

population (pop′yə lā′shən), all the organisms of one species that live in a certain place.

product (prod′əkt), a substance that is formed in a chemical reaction.

psychrometer (sī krom′ə tər), an instrument used to measure relative humidity.

purebred (pyür′bred′), an organism with two dominant or two recessive genes for a trait.

Q

quasar (kwā′sär), brilliant object in space that may be the powerhouses of developing galaxies.

R

reactant (rē ak′tənt), a substance that undergoes a chemical reaction, often by combining with another substance.

recessive gene (re ses′iv jēn), a gene whose expression is prevented by a dominant gene.

red giant (red jī′ənt), a star that has swelled and glows with a red color.

red shift (red shift), the change of light waves from retreating objects to the red end of the spectrum.

reflex (rē′fleks), quick, automatic response to a stimulus.

refraction (ri frak′shən), the bending of a light wave as it moves from one material to another.

relative humidity (rel′ə tiv hyü mid′ə tē), measurement that compares the amount of water vapor in the air with the amount air can hold at a certain temperature.

relative motion (rel′ə tiv mō′shən), the change in position of one object compared to the position of another.

renewable resource (ri nü′ə bəl ri sôrs′), a resource that can be replaced within a reasonably short time.

reservoir (rez′ər vwär), artificial lake used to collect and store water.

respiration (res′pə rā′shən), energy-producing process in which a cell combines oxygen with sugars and gives off carbon dioxide and water.

response (ri spons′), a reaction of an organism to a change in the environment.

retina (ret′nə), an area at the back of the eye that contains sensory receptors for light.

ribosome (rī′bə sōm), organelle that puts together proteins for the cell.

Richter scale (rik′tər skāl), a scale used to compare the strengths of earthquakes.

S

saltwater biome (sôlt′wô′tər bī′ōm) water biome that has high salt content.

sediment (sed′ə mənt), rock and soil carried by water.

seismograph (sīz′mə graf), instrument that records the strengths of the earth's movements, based on the amount of energy released.

sensory neuron (sen′sər ē nür′on), nerve cell in the peripheral nervous system that carries information from sensory receptors to the CNS.

sensory receptor (sen′sər ē ri sep′tər), cell within the peripheral nervous system that gathers information from the environment and from the inside of the body.

sex cell (seks sel), a type of cell produced only by an organism that reproduces sexually.

sexual reproduction (sek′shü əl rē prə duk′shən), reproduction by two parents.

side effect (sīd ə fekt′), unwanted effect of a medicine or drug.

smokeless tobacco (smōk′lis tə bak′ō), tobacco, such as chewing tobacco or snuff, that is not smoked when it is used.

soil profile (soil prō′fil), layers of soil in an area.

solar eclipse (sō′lər i klips′), an alignment of the sun, moon, and Earth where the moon blocks the sun from Earth's view.

solar energy (sō′lər en ər jē), radiant energy that comes from the sun.

solar flare (sō′lər fler), powerful eruption of very hot gases from the sun.

solstice (sol′stis), a point in the Earth's orbit around the sun where daylight is either the longest or shortest amount possible.

solute (sol′yüt), a substance that is dissolved.

solvent (sol′vənt), a substance that dissolves other materials.

sonar (sō′när), a device that uses sound waves to measure distance.

species (spē′shēz), a group of organisms that have the same characteristics and are able to produce offspring that can reproduce.

speed (spēd), the distance an object moves in a certain period of time.

speedometer (spē dom′ə tər), a device that shows instantaneous speed.

spinal cord (spī′nl kord), bundle of neurons that carries messages back and forth between the brain and the rest of the body.

stewardship (stü′ərd ship), the taking care of Earth's resources to ensure their quality and quantity for future generations.

stimulant (stim′yōō lənt), a drug that speeds up the nervous system.

stimulus (stim′yə ləs), a change in the environment of an organism that causes a response.

structural adaptation (struk′cher əl ad′ap tā′shən), adaptation that involves body parts or color.

sunspot (sun′spot′), a region on the sun of very strong magnetic fields.

supernova (sü′pər nō′və), the explosion of a star, releasing huge amounts of light and other energy.

synapse (si naps′), the gap between the axon of one neuron and the dendrite of a second neuron.

T

taiga (tī′gə), forest biome just south of the tundra, characterized by conifers.

tar (tär), a sticky, gluelike substance found in cigarette smoke.

tides (tīdz), the rise and fall of water in the ocean and seas caused mainly by the gravitational pull of the moon on the earth.

tornado (tôr nā′dō), a violent, funnel-shaped cloud with extremely strong winds.

trait (trāt), a characteristic of an organism.

transparent (tran spər′ənt), allows light to pass through so that objects on the other side can be seen.

transverse wave (trans vėrs′ wāv), a wave in which the crests and troughs move at right angles to the direction of the wave's travel.

tundra (tun′drə), the northernmost and coldest biome.

V

vacuole (vak′yü ōl), saclike organelle used for storing materials.

velocity (və los′ə tē), a measure of both the speed and direction of a moving object.

vent (vent), opening on the ocean floor.

W

water table (wô′tər tā′bəl), the top of an aquifer.

weathering (weᴛʜ′ər ing), group of processes that break rocks into smaller pieces.

weight (wāt), a measure of the pull of gravity on an object's mass.

Z

zygote (zī′gōt), the first cell of an offspring, formed when an egg cell and sperm cell join.

Index

A

Acceleration, B92–93, B102–103

Acid rain, B66–67

Acid, B62–63, B67–68

Activities
   Explore, A6, A38, A74, A112, B6, B32, B76, B116, C6, C42, C80, C110, D6, D34
   Investigate, A14, A24, A60, A68, A98, A106, A122, A146, B18, B26, B48, B60, B100, B110, B130, B152, C26, C52, C66, C98, C126, D18, D42
   Experiment, A31, B69, C135, D27

Adaptations, A78–79
   behavioral, A100
   physiological, A96–97
   structural, A88
   species and, A88

Addiction, D38

Air mass, C28

Air pressure, C11
   wind and, C11

Air resistance, B97–98, B104–105

Alchemists, B42

Alcohol abuse, D54–55

Alcohol, D52
   amounts in drinks, D53
   effects on body, D52–53
   choosing not to use, D57

Alcoholics, D56

Alcoholism, D56

Alternate energy sources, C132

Ameba, A29, A44, A97

Anemometer, C20

Aneroid barometer, C21

Aquifer, C60

Archaeopteryx, C72

Aristotle, B104, C18

Asexual reproduction, A44–45
   ameba, A44
   bacteria, A44
   yeast, A44

Astronaut, C102, C105

Atmosphere
   composition of air, A126, C115
   layers of, 36

Atoms, B50, 37
   and fusion, C88

Auroras, C90

Automated surface observing systems, C30

Axon, D20–21

B

Bacteria, A28, A29, A44, A93, A126, C121

Barometer, C19

Base (chemical), B63, B67–68

Base (DNA), A54

Behavior
   imprinting, A105
   inherited, A102–103
   learned, A104–105

Big bang theory, C97

Biome, A136
   altitude and, A136
   climate and, A136
   land, A138–145
   water, A148–153

Black dwarf, C95

Black hole, C96

Blood
   platelets, A43

red blood cells, A27, A43
white blood cells, A27, A28, A43
Boiling point, B38
Boyle, Robert, B140
Brain stem, D11
Brain, D9–12

C

Caffeine, D38–39
Cancer, D47
Carbon cycle, C115
Carbon monoxide, D46
Carnivores, A116
Cell membrane, A17, A19, C21
Cell theory, A13
Cell wall, A21
Cells, A8, A10, A16–21, A26
   animal, A16–19
   differences, A26–30
   discovery of, A10–11
   plant, A20–21
   parts of A16–21
Celsius, Anders, B12
Central nervous system, D9–12
Cerebellum, D10
Cerebrum, D10
Chemical bond, B51
Chemical equation, B58–59
Chemical formula, B58
Chemical reaction, B51–52
   product, B5
   reactant, B51
   types of, B53–55
Chemical symbol, B58
Chlorophyll, A20, A22
Chloroplast, A20, A21

Chromosome, A16, A19, A40, A46, A50–51,
   A52, A63
Cilia, A28
Circuits, 31
Circulatory system, D53, 39
   effects of alcohol on, D53
   effects of smoking on, D46
Cirrhosis, D54
Classifying, xiv–xv, 10–11
   clouds, C14–15
   living things, 30
Clouds, C14
   classification of, C14–15
   formation of, C14
   precipitation and, C16–17
Collecting and interpreting data, xiv–xv,
   24–25
Color
   primary colors of light, B135
   primary colors of paint, B136
   seeing, B134–139
Communicating, xiv–xv, 8–9
Competition, A132
Compound microscope, A10
Compounds, B51, B53, B58
Condensation, B39
   dew point and, C13
Conduction, B20–21, B24-25
Conductors, B20–21
Cones, B134, D14
Conservation 0f mass, B59
Conservation, C132
Consumers, A116–116
Contraction, B14–17
Convection, B22–25
   Earth's plate movements and, C45
   within the sun, C88

Corona, C88–89

Crick, Francis, A53

Crocodile, A101

Cycles
  nitrogen, A126-127
  oxygen-carbon dioxide A124–125
   pollution and, A128–129

Cytoplasm, A17, A19, A20, A21

D

Darwin, Charles, A84–87

DaVinci, Leonardo, B118

Decibel scale, B144

Decomposers, A117

Dendrite, D20–22

Depressant, D39

Desert, A145

Dew point, C13

Digestive system, 38

Dinosaur extinction, C73

Disease, A43, A44

Displacement, B89

Distance, B88–89

DNA, A52
  duplication, A56–57
  DNA sequence, A58
  genetic fingerprinting, A59
  mutations, A67
  structure, A53–55

Doctor, D37

Dopplar radar, C23

Drainage basin, C58

Drug abuse, D38, D41

Drug, D36

E

Ear (human), B145, D15, D17

Earth
  crust of, C44–46, C68–74
  movement of, C82–85

Earthquakes, C47
  predicting, C50–51

Echo, B146

Ecosystems, A114
  changes within, A130–131, A134–135
  field, A118119, A120
  park, A114–115
  pond, A119
  prairie, A132–133

Egg cell, A46, A48, A63

El Nino, A131

Electromagnetic spectrum, B132–134
  space objects and, C101
  visible spectrum, B133

Electron, 37

Elements, B50–51, B53, B58

Emphysema, D46

Endocrine glands, D24

Endocrine system, D24–26, 39

Endoplasmic reticulum, A18, A19, A21

Endothermic reactions, B57

Energy
  chemical reactions and, B56–57
  earthquakes and, C47–48
  ecosystems and, A118–121
  fossil fuels and, C118
  friction and, B97
  fusion and, C88
  life processes, A23, A76–77, A116
  ocean waves and, C62
  particle movement and, B9
  states of matter and, B35–39
  sun and, A20, A22, C87–88

thermal, B9
transformations, 32
uses of, B56
waves and, B120–121
Energy pyramid, A120-121
Equinox, C85
Estimating and Measuring, xiv–xv, 12–13
Estuary, A152
Evaporation, B38–39, C119
Evolution,
   Charles Darwin and,
   evidence of, A82–83
   mutations and, A82
Excretion, A77
Exothermic reaction, B56–57
Expansion, B14–17
Experimenting, xiv–xv, 28–29
Eye (human), D14, D17

F

Fahrenheit, Gabriel, B12
Feedback loop, D25–26
Fertilization, A48, A63
Fiber optics, B125
Firefighters, C9
Flagella, A29
Focus, C47
Food chain, A118
Food web, A118–119
Force, B78–79
   acceleration and, B102
   action and reaction, B106–107
   balanced and unbalanced, B83–85
   gravity, B80–81
   net force, B84–85
   weight, B82

Formulating questions and hypothesis,
   xiv–xv, 22–23
Fossil fuels, C118, C132
Fossils, A80–84
   formation of, A80, C70
   types of, A80
   use of, A81–83, C70–74
Freezing point, B37
Freshwater
   biome, A150–151
   resources, C124–125
Friction, B97–B98
Frog, A49
Front, C29
Fuel, B57, C118, C121
Fujita, T. Theodore, C35
Fusion, C88

G

Galapagos Islands, A84–86
Galaxies, C91–92
Galilei, Galileo, B94, B104, C19
Gene, A53–55, A57
   blending, A64
   dominant and recessive, A64–66
   heredity, A63
   protein production, A57
   traits, A53, A63–A66
Genome, A58
Geologic time scale, C74
Geostationary satellites, C25
Geothermal energy, C132
Glaciers, C64–65
Global warming, C131
Grassland, A144

Gravity, B80
    mass and, B81, B104
    moon and tides, B80
    motion and, B95
Groundwater, C60–61
Guard cells, A26, A96

H

Hallucinogens, D40
Heat, B8–10
    expansion and contraction, B14–15
    flow of energy and, B8–10
    temperature and, B10–11
Herbivores, A116
Heredity, A63
Hertz, B143
History of science, A10, A13, A53, A84,
    A86, B12, B42, B94, B104, B118, B122,
    B128, B132, C18, C50, C72, C74, C104,
    D37, 44–55
Hooke, Robert, A10, A13, A21
Hormone, D24
Hubble Space Telescope, C101
Human Genome Project, A58
Humidity, C12
    temperature and, C13
Hurricane, C36
Huygens, Christian, B119
Hybrid, A65
Hypothalamus, D11

I

Identifying and controlling variables, xiv–xv,
    26–27
Index fossil, C71
Indicators, B65
Inertia, B95–96, B99, B104

Inferring, xiv–xv, 14–15
Inhalant, D40
Instinct, A102–103
Insulators, B21
Intoxicated, D53
Ion, B62–B63
Ionosphere, 36

J

Janssen, Hans, A10
Janssen, Zaccharias, A10

K

Keck Telescope, C100–101

L

Langevin, Paul, B146
Lasers, B128–129, C51
Law, B94
Laws of motion, Newton's, B94
    first law of motion, B94–105, B108
    second law of motion, B102–105, B109
    third law of motion, B106–107, B109
Lenses,
    concave, B127
    convex, B127
    focal point, B127
    uses of, B127
Lenses, A10
Life processes, A76–77
Light, B118
    as particles and waves, B118–119
    reflection, B122–125
    refraction, B126–127
    visible, B133
    opaque objects, B136
    transparent objects, B138
Lightning, C34

Lithosphere, C44

Local Group, C92

Lou Gehrig's disease, D22

Lunar eclipse, C86

M

Machines, 33

Magnets, B56

Marijuana, D50
  effects on body, D50, D51

Mass, B81
  acceleration and, B102

Math in Science
  Bar Graphs, A7
  Metric conversions, A39
  Positive and Negative Numbers, B7
  Measuring Angles, B117
  Percent, C7
  Large Numbers, C81
  Rate, D7

Medicine, D36–37
  using safely, D37
  labels, D36
  side effects, D37

Meiosis, A46–48, A50–51

Melting point, B36

Mesosphere, 36

Meteorologist, C9, C22, C28

Microscope, A11, 41
  compound microscope, A10–12
  electron microscope, A12
  parts of A11

Milky Way Galaxy, C91–92

Minerals, B138, C117, C120, C121

Mirrors,
  concave, B124
  convex, B124
  uses of, B124–125

Mitochondria, A18, A19, A21, A22

Mitosis, A40–41, A43, A50–51
  cell division, A40
  growth, A42
  repair, A43

Models, xiv–xv, 20–21

Molecule, B51, 37

Moon
  orbit of, C85
  phases of, C85

Moraine, C64

Morse, Samuel F. B., C19

Motion, B86–B87, B94
  changes in, B94–96
  forces, B95
  friction, B97
  types, B86–87

Motor neurons, D13, D21

Multiple sclerosis, D22

Muscle
  cells, A27

Muscular system, 39

Music, B148–151

Mutation,
  evolution and, A82

N

Natural selection, A86–87

Nebula, C93

Neptune, B36, B38

Nerve cells (neuron), A27, D9

Nerve impulse, D20–23

Nervous system, D8–13, 38
  effects of alcohol on, D54
  effects of depressants on, D39
  effects of hallucinogens on, D40
  effects of stimulants on, D38

Neutralization reactions, B67–68

Neutron star, C96

Neutron, 37

Newton (measurement), B92

Newton, Sir Isaac, B94, B95, B118, B132

Nicotine, D44, D46

Nitrogen cycle, A126–127, A129, C116

Nodule, C120

Noise, B148–151

Nose (human), D16, D17

Nova, C95

Nuclear power, C133

Nucleus, A16, A19, A40

O

Observatories, C101

Observing, xiv–xv, 6–7

Ocean
  resources, C120–123
  waves, C62–63

Octave, B149,

Oil
  ocean resource, C121–122
  drilling, C122

Omnivores, A116

Operational definitions, xiv–xv, 18–19

Ore, C117

Organelle, A18

Oxygen-carbon dioxide cycle, A124, A128, C115

P

Paleontologist, A81

Paracelsus, Phillipus, B42

Parkinson's disease, D22

Peppered moths, A89

Periodic table of the elements, 42–43

Peripheral nervous system, D9, D12–13

Permafrost, A140

pH
  effects on environment, B66
  scale, B64

Pharmacist, D37

Photon, B119

Photosynthesis, A22, A116, A124–125

Pistil, A50

Pitch, B143

Planets, C82, 35

Plankton, C123

Plastids, A21

Plate boundaries, C46

Plate tectonics, C44–46, C49

Pollen, A50

Pollutant, C130

Pollution, A128–129, C130–131

Population, A90
  human, A134

Precipitation, C16–17, C119

Predicting, xiv–xv, 16–17

Process Skills, xiv–xv, , 6–29
  Classifying, 10–11
  Collecting and Interpreting Data, 24–25
  Communicating, 8–9
  Estimating and Measuring, 12–13
  Experimenting, 28–29
  Formulating Questions and Hypotheses, 22–23
  Identifying and controlling Variables, 26–27
  Inferring, 14–15
  Making and Using Models, 20-–21
  Making Operational Definitions, 18–19
  Observing, 6–7
  Predicting, 16–17

Producers, A116–117

Proton, 37

Pseudopod, A29

Psychrometer, C21

Purebred, A65

Q

Quasars, C92

R

Radiation, B23–25

Reading for Science
Comparing and Contrasting, C111
Drawing Conclusions, A75
Identifying Cause and Effect, B77
Making Predictions, A113
Supporting Facts and Details, D35
Using Context Clues, B33
Using Graphic Sources, C43

Recycling, C143

Red giant, C94

Red shift, C97

Reflecting telescope, C100

Reflex, A103, D22–23

Relative humidity, C13

Relative motion, B38
frame of reference, B85

Reproduction, A77

Reservoir, C124

Resources
conserving, C132–134
human impact on, C113–114, C128–133
in air, C115–116
on land, C117–118
protecting, C130–131
renewable/nonrenewable, C112–113

Respiration, A22, A124–125

Respiratory system, D45, 38
effects of smoking on, D45–46

Response, A92–93
bacteria, A93
human, A93
plant, A93, A96–A97
ptarmigan, A92
seal, A96

Retina, D14

Retina, D14

Ribosome, A18, A19, A21

Richter scale, C48

Richter, Charles, C48

Rivers, C57–58
as sculptors of land, C58–59

Rock cycle, 34

Rocks, C68–69, C73, 34

Rods, B134, D14

S

Safety in Science, 2–3

Salt, B68, C120

Saltwater biome, A148–149

Schleiden, Matthias, A13

Schwann, Theodore, A13

Scientific methods, xii–xiii, A31, B69, C135, D27

Scientific tools, 40–41
balance, 40
graduated cylinder, 40
meter stick, 41
microscope, A10–12, 41
spring scale, 41
thermometer, B12–B13, C21, 40

Seasons, C84

Secondhand smoke, D47

Sediment, C58

Seed, A50

Seismograph, C48, C50

Senses, A94–95

Sensory neurons, D13, D21

Sensory receptors, D12–13, D22

Sex cells, A46

Sexual reproduction, A46–49
    alligator, A49
    frog, A48–49
    mammals, A49
    plants, A50

Skeletal system, 39

Skin, D16, D17
    cells A27

Soil, C54–56
    as a resource, C117
    conservation of
    differences in, C56
    formation of, C55
    pH, B66

Solar eclipse, C89

Solar energy, C133

Solar flares, C90

Solar system, C82–83, C92, 35

Solstice, C84

Solute, B41

Solutions, B40
    concentrated and dilute, B44
    dissolving, B40, B45–47
    types, B43
    uses, B42

Solvent, B41

Sonar, B146–147

Sound, B140
    differences, B42–143
    ear and, D15
    energy of, B142
    intensity, B144
    loudness, B144
    pitch, B143
    reflection, B146–147

refraction, B147
    travel, B140

Space exploration, C103–105
    history of, C104–105
    technology from, C103

Space probes, C102

Space shuttles, C102

Space station, C102

Species, A8–9
    evolution of, A90–A91

Speed, B90–93
    instantaneous speed, B91

Speedometer, B91

Sperm cell, A46, A48, A63

Spider, A101, A103

Spinal cord, D11–12

Stamen, A50

Stars
    fusion and, C88
    life cycle, C93–96

States of matter, B34-36

Stewardship, C128–128

Stimulant, D38–39

Stimulus, A92–93

Storms
    types of, C34

Stratosphere, 36

Sun, C87–90
    fusion and, C88

Sunspots, C89–90

Supernova, C95–96

Synapse, D21

T

Taiga, A141

Tar, D46

Temperate deciduous forest, A142

Temperature, B10
    heat and, B10
    humidity and, C12
    measuring, B12–B13
    states of matter and, B34–39
Thermogram, B13
Thermometer, B12–13, C21, 40
Thermosphere, 36
Thermostat, B17
Tidal power, C133
Tides, B80, C86
Tiltmeter, C51
Tobacco, D44
    choosing not to use, D48
    effects of smoking on body, D45–48
    smokeless, D44, D48
Tongue (human), D16, D17
Tornado, C35–C36
Torricelli, Evangelista, C19
Trait,
    adaptation, A78
    DNA, A52, A55,
    mutations, A67
Transportation, C119
Trilobites, C73
Tropical rain forest, A143
Tundra, A140

U

Ultrasound, B145

V

Vacuole, A18, A19, A20, A21
van Leeuwenhoek, Anton, A10
Velocity, B91–B93
Vents (hot water ocean), A117, C121
Venus, B36

Virchow, Rudolph, A13
Volcanoes, C49
    Pompeii, C50
    predicting, C50–51
Volvox, A29
von Frisch, Karl, B134
Vorticella, A28

W

Water
    expansion and contraction, B15
Water cycle, C119
Water table, C60
Watson, James, A53
Waves, B120
    characteristics of, B120–121
    compressional, B141–142
    transverse, B121
Weather forecasts
    safety and, C9–10, C37
    history of, C18–C19, C22–25
    instruments for, C20–25, C30–31
Weather maps, C32–33
Weather satellites, C24–25
Weathering, C55
Weight, B92
White dwarf, C95
Writing for Science,
    Using Graphic Organizers, A160
    Organizing Information, B160
    Using Reference Sources, C144
    Reading a Table, D64

Y

Yeast, A44

Z

Zygote, A48, A50, A63

Acknowledgments

Illustration

Borders Patti Green
Icons Precison Graphics

Unit A
8a John Zielinski
17 Carla Kiwior
19 Christine D. Young
21 Christine D. Young
22 Precision Graphics
41 Barbara Cousins
44 Vilma Ortiz-Dillon
47 Barbara Cousins
53 Barbara Cousins
54 Barbara Cousins
56 Barbara Cousins
58a Barbara Cousins
59 John Zielinski
63 Barbara Cousins
64 Richard Stergulz
65 Richard Stergulz
78 Barbara Harmon
82 Richard Stergulz
84 Precision Graphics
88 Carla Kiwior
90 Walter Stuart
91 Walter Stuart
114 Meryl Treatner
119 Carla Kiwior
120 Michael Digiorgio
121 Michael Digiorgio
124b Precision Graphics
126a Precision Graphics
128 Precision Graphics
130a Carla Kiwior
137a Precision Graphics
137b Michael Carroll
137c Michael Carroll
138 Precision Graphics
149 Carla Kiwior
150 Carla Kiwior
151 Carla Kiwior
152 Carla Kiwior
158 Barbara Cousins, Steven Edsey & Sons.

Unit B
12 Rob Schuster
15 J/B Woolsey
17 Michael Carroll
23 George Hamblin
34 J/B Woolsey
36 J/B Woolsey
38 J/B Woolsey
40 J/B Woolsey
44 J/B Woolsey
51 J/B Woolsey
58 Kenneth Batelman
65 Dave Merrill
86 John Massie
89 Kenneth Batelman
90 Walter Stuart
93 Precision Graphics
99 J/B Woolsey
107 Pedro Gonzalez
120 Kenneth Batelman
121 George Hamblin
122 J/B Woolsey
123 J/B Woolsey
124 J/B Woolsey
125 J/B Woolsey
127 J/B Woolsey
135 Kenneth Batelman
136 Kenneth Batelman
137 Michael Carroll
141 J/B Woolsey
142 J/B Woolsey
143 Michael Carroll
145 John Massie
147 Michael Carroll
150 Michael Carroll
151 Kenneth Batelman

Unit C
8 Kenneth Batelman
11 J/B Woolsey
12 Jared Schneidman
13 J/B Woolsey
14 Precision Graphics
16 Precision Graphics
21 John Zielinski
23 Michael Carroll
28 Precision Graphics
31 Precision Graphics
33 Precision Graphics
45a Precision Graphics
45b Nadine Sokol
47 Alan Cormack
48 George Hamblin
49 Alan Cormack
55 J/B Woolsey
58 J/B Woolsey
59 J/B Woolsey
60 Michael Carroll
62 Carla Kiwior
64 Precision Graphics
70 Nadine Sokol
71 Michael Digiorgio
72 Carla Kiwior
74 Precision Graphics
82 J/B Woolsey
84 J/B Woolsey
85 J/B Woolsey
86 J/B Woolsey
88 J/B Woolsey
89 J/B Woolsey
92 J/B Woolsey
94 J/B Woolsey
96 J/B Woolsey
100 John Zielinski
119 Precision Graphics
122 Michael Digiorgio
131 J/B Woolsey
133 Precision Graphics
143 J/B Woolsey

Unit D
9 Joel Ito
11 Rodd Ambroson
14 Rodd Ambroson
15 Rodd Ambroson
16 Rodd Ambroson
20 Christine D. Young
23 Joel Ito
24 Joel Ito
45 Joel Ito
52 Joel Ito

Photography

Unless otherwise credited, all photographs are the property of Scott Foresman, a division of Pearson Education. Page abbreviations are as follows: (T) top, (C) center, (B) bottom, (L) left, (R) right, (INS) inset.

Cover: Roda/Natural Selection Stock Photography, Inc.

iv BR M. Abbey/Visuals Unlimited
v TR Joe McDonald/Animals Animals/Earth Scenes
ix TR PhotoDisc, Inc

Unit A
1 Kenneth Edward/Photo Researchers
2 T Vincent O'Bryne/Panoramic Images
2 B-inset-2 Mark C. Burnett/Photo Researchers
2 C Dan McCoy/Rainbow
2 B Arie deZanger for Scott Foresman
2 B-inset 1 Photo Researchers
3 B J. F. Podevin/Image Bank
3 TCR NASA/SPL/Photo Researchers
3 BCR G. I. Bernard/Animals Animals/Earth Scenes
9 C Eddy Gray/SPL/SSC/Photo Researchers
9 BL Rod Planck/TOM STACK & ASSOCIATES
9 TR Steven David Miller/Animals Animals/Earth Scenes
9 BR Mike Bacon/TOM STACK & ASSOCIATES
9 TL Bruce Watkins/Animals Animals/Earth Scenes
10 B Cecil Fox/SS/Photo Researchers
10 T Science VU/Visuals Unlimited
12 T Jan Hinsch/SPL/SSC/Photo Researchers
12 B David Parker/SPL/SSC/Photo Researchers
12 C Andrew Syred/SPL/SSC/Photo Researchers
13 T Mike Abbey/Visuals Unlimited
13 B Anthony Bannister/Animals Animals/Earth Scenes
16 Profesors P. Motta & T. Naguro/SPL/SSC/Photo Researchers
18 Professor P. Motta/Dept. of Anatomy/University "La Sapienza", Rome/SPL/SSC/Photo Researchers
20 M. Eichelberger/Visuals Unlimited
23 T Superstock, Inc.
23 B S. Maslowski/Visuals Unlimited
26 B Ray Coleman/NASC/Photo Researchers
26 T John D. Cunningham/Visuals Unlimited
27 TL David M. Phillips/Visuals Unlimited
27 TR Superstock, Inc.
27 BL Oliver Meckes/Ottawa/SPL/SSC/Photo Researchers
27 BR Professors P. M. Andrews/K.R. Porter and J. Vial/SSC/Photo Researchers
28 CL M. Abbey/Visuals Unlimited
28 BL Stan Flegler/Visuals Unlimited
28 BR Cabisco/Visuals Unlimited
29 B Malcolm Boulton/Photo Researchers
29 T Gopal Murti/CNRI/Phototake
30 T Profesor P. Motta/Dept. of Anatomy/University "La Sapienza", Rome/SPL/SSC/Photo Researchers
30 B K. Aufderheide/Visuals Unlimited
35 S. Maslowski/Visuals Unlimited
40 David M. Phillips/Visuals Unlimited
42 T Scott Brenner/Ken IWagner/Visuals Unlimited
42 B PhotoDisc, Inc.
43 T Dr. E. R. Degginger/Color-Pic, Inc.
43 B David M. Phillips/Visuals Unlimited
44 BL J. Forsdyke/Gene Cox/SPL/Photo Researchers
44 BC Biophoto Associates/Photo Researchers
44 BR Biophoto Associates/Photo Researchers
44 T Oliver Meckes/Photo Researchers
45 R Biophoto Associates/Photo Researchers
45 L Biophoto Associates/Photo Researchers
46 David M. Phillips/Photo Researchers
48 BL VU/Cabisco/Visuals Unlimited
48 BR VU/Cabisco/Visuals Unlimited
49 T Chris Johns/Tony Stone Images
49 BL VU/Cabisco/Visuals Unlimited
49 BR VU/Cabisco/Visuals Unlimited
50 T PhotoDisc, Inc.
50 B G. Thomas Bishop/Custom Medical Stock Photo
52 M. P. Kahl/Photo Researchers
58 BR David Parker/SPL/Photo Researchers
62 Walter Hodges/Tony Stone Images
62 Background PhotoDisc, Inc.
67 T Joe McDonald/Visuals Unlimited
67 B Alex Kerstitch/Visuals Unlimited
71 Chris Johns/Tony Stone Images
75 L Lynn Stone/Animals Animals/Earth Scenes
75 C Leonard Lee Rue III/Photo Researchers
75 R Francois Gohier/Photo Researchers
76 Jeff Lepore/Photo Researchers
77 T Francois Gohier/Photo Researchers
77 B Michael Fogden/Animals Animals/Earth Scenes
77 C Anthony Bannister/Animals Animals/Earth Scenes
79 L Lynn Stone/Animals Animals/Earth Scenes
79 R Francois Gohier/Photo Researchers
79 C Leonard Lee Rue III/Photo Researchers
80 Don W. Fawcett/Visuals Unlimited
81 B J. Koivula/SS/Photo Researchers

81 C Joe McDonald/Animals Animals/Earth Scenes
81 T James L. Amos/Photo Researchers
85 T Ken Lucas/Visuals Unlimited
85 B Michael Dick/Animals Animals/Earth Scenes
86 The Granger Collection, New York
86 Background MetaPhotos
87 BR J.W. Verderber/Visuals Unlimited
87 TR Hal Beral/Visuals Unlimited
87 TL Alex Kerstitch/Visuals Unlimited
89 T Breck P. Kent/Animals Animals/Earth Scenes
92 L Jan L. Wassink/Visuals Unlimited
92 R David C. Fritts/Animals Animals/Earth Scenes
94 T James Watt/Animals Animals/Earth Scenes
94 B PhotoDisc, Inc.
95 T C. P. Hickman/Visuals Unlimited
95 C E. R. Degginger/Animals Animals/Earth Scenes
95 B Chris McLaughlin/Animals Animals/Earth Scenes
96 B Howard Hall/OSF/Animals Animals/Earth Scenes
96 T Andrew Syred/SPL/Photo Researchers
97 B Adrienne T. Gibson/Animals Animals/Earth Scenes
97 T M. Abbey/Visuals Unlimited
100 Fred Bruemmer
101 T Jonathan Blair/National Geographic Image Collection
101 B J. Alcock/Visuals Unlimited
101 C N. M. Collins/OSF/Animals Animals/Earth Scenes
102 L Lee F. Snyder/Photo Researchers
102 R Francis Lepine/Animals Animals/Earth Scenes
103 T J. A. L. Cooke/Animals Animals/Earth Scenes
104 Charles Gupton/Tony Stone Images
105 Alfred B. Thomas/Animals Animals/Earth Scenes
109 Lee F. Snyder/Photo Researchers
113 T PhotoDisc, Inc.
113 TC Rod Planck/Photo Researchers
113 BC J. H. Robinson/Photo Researchers
113 B Renee Lynn/Photo Researchers
116 E. R. Degginger/Color-Pic, Inc.
117 B WHOI/D.Foster/Visuals Unlimited
117 T Stanley Flegler/Visuals Unlimited
118 B Renee Lynn/Photo Researchers
118 BC J. H. Robinson/Photo Researchers
118 TC Rod Planck/Photo Researchers
118 T PhotoDisc, Inc.
126 Oliver Meckes/Photo Researchers
127 Cabisco/Visuals Unlimited
131 T Len Zell/OSF/Animals Animals/Earth Scenes
131 B F. Stuart Westmorland/Photo Researchers
132 T Stephen Dalton/Photo Researchers
132 B Mark Stouffer/Animals Animals/Earth Scenes
133 T Fritz Polking/Visuals Unlimited
134 T Charlie Ott/Photo Researchers
134 B Paul A. Grecian/Visuals Unlimited
134 B-Inset Andrew Martinez/Photo Researchers
135 C Pat Armstrong/Visuals Unlimited
135 T Courtesy General Motors Corporation/Wieck Photo DataBase
136 B PhotoDisc, Inc.
136 T PhotoDisc, Inc.
138 L Stephen J. Krasemann/Photo Researchers
138 R Robert W. Domm/Visuals Unlimited
138 C Doug Sokell/Visuals Unlimited
139 C Gary Braasch/Tony Stone Images
139 R David Matherly/Visuals Unlimited
139 L Ron Spomer/Visuals Unlimited
140 B-Inset Alan D. Carey/Photo Researchers
140 T Stephen J. Krasemann/Photo Researchers
140 B Jim Zipp/Photo Researchers
141 B E. R. Degginger/Color-Pic, Inc.
141 T Doug Sokell/Visuals Unlimited
142 CC Phil Degginger/Animals Animals/Earth Scenes
142 B North Wind Picture Archives
142 TC Patti Murray/Animals Animals/Earth Scenes
142 T Robert W. Domm/Visuals Unlimited
143 B Andy Sacks/Tony Stone Images
143 T Ron Spomer/Visuals Unlimited

144 T Gary Braasch/Tony Stone Images
144 B Superstock
144 B-INSET Cabisco/Visuals Unlimited
145 TL David Matherly/Visuals Unlimited
145 B E. R. Degginger/Color-Pic, Inc.
145 TR John Chard/Tony Stone Images
148 NASA
152 E. R. Degginger/Color-Pic, Inc.
153 PhotoDisc, Inc.
155 F. Stuart Westmorland/Photo Researchers
156 BL VU/Cabisco/Visuals Unlimited
156 BC VU/Cabisco/Visuals Unlimited
156 BR VU/Cabisco/Visuals Unlimited
157 Michael Fogden/Animals Animals/Earth Scenes
159 B J. Forsdyke/Gene Cox/SPL/Photo Researchers
159 T PhotoDisc, Inc.

Unit B
1 D. Boone/Corbis-Westlight
2 T Vincent O'Bryne/Panoramic Images
2 BL Arie deZanger for Scott Foresman
3 C Nicholas Pinturas/Tony Stone Images
11 T Arthur Tilley/FPG International Corp.
13 Dan McCoy/Rainbow
14 L Richard Megna/Fundamental Photographs
14 R Richard Megna/Fundamental Photographs
15 L Richard Megna/Fundamental Photographs
15 R Richard Megna/Fundamental Photographs
15 C Richard Megna/Fundamental Photographs
15 L Richard Megna/Fundamental Photographs
16 T Jill Birschbach
16 B William Wright/Fundamental Photographs
17 Dr. E. R. Degginger/Color-Pic, Inc.
21 R Randy Green/FPG International LLC
21 L Nancy Sheehan/PhotoEdit
24 James Schwabel/Panoramic Images
28 Randy Green/FPG International LLC
29 NASA/SS/Photo Researchers
33 Steve Satushek/Image Bank
35 Steve Kaufman/Corbis Media
36 NASA
37 Carr Clifton/Minden Pictures
38 David Young-Wolff/PhotoEdit
39 Steve Satushek/Image Bank
42 B Brooks/Brown/SSC/Photo Researchers
43 C Jeremy Burgess/Photo Researchers
50 L Boltin Picture Library
50 R Boltin Picture Library
50 BC Charles D. Winters/Photo Researchers
50 CC John Cancalosi/TOM STACK & ASSOCIATES
53 T Kal's Power Tools
54 T UPI/Corbis-Bettmann
55 B Lawrence Migdale/Photo Researchers
56 T E. R. Degginger/NASC/Photo Researchers
56 B Superstock, Inc.
59 PhotoDisc, Inc.
63 TR PhotoDisc, Inc.
63 CL PhotoDisc, Inc.
63 CR PhotoDisc, Inc.
65 T USDA Nature Source/Photo Researchers
66 T Gilbert S. Grant/NASC/Photo Researchers
66 C Michael Boys/Corbis Media
66 B Kevin R. Morris/Corbis Media
67 B Superstock, Inc.
67 T Peter Miller/NASC/Photo Researchers
68 Scott T. Smith/Corbis Media
78 Oxford Scientific Films/Animals Animals/Earth Scenes
79 T Mike Hewitt/Allsport
80 BL Akira Fujii
80 BR Craig J. Brown/Liaison Agency
80 T David Madison/Tony Stone Images
81 Tim Davis/Tony Stone Images
82 L NASA
82 R Akira Fujii
85 John Warden/Tony Stone Images
87 Jose Carrillo/PhotoEdit
88 Mark Wagner/Tony Stone Images
90 Laguna Photo/Liaison Agency
92 Tony Freeman/PhotoEdit
94 N. Pecnik/Visuals Unlimited
95 Jonathan Daniel/Allsport
96 L Don Smetzer/Tony Stone Images

96 R Joe Caputo/Liaison Agency
97 Novastock/PhotoEdit
105 Joseph McBride/Tony Stone Images
106 Jonathan Nourok/PhotoEdit
108 L Dan McCoy/Rainbow
108 R E. R. Degginger/Color-Pic, Inc.
109 T VCG/FPG International Corp.
109 B Jose Carrillo/PhotoEdit
118 Novastock/PhotoEdit
120 Vince Streano/Tony Stone Images
123 PhotoDisc, Inc.
124 Warren Stone/Visuals Unlimited
125 Spencer Grant/Photo Researchers
129 B Scott Camazine/Photo Researchers
129 T Rosenfeld Images LTD/SPL/Photo Researchers
132 David Parker/Photo Researchers
135 B Novastock/PhotoEdit
135 C Jerome Wexler/Photo Researchers
137 B Gregg Hadel/Tony Stone Images
138 R Paul Silverman/Fundamental Photographs
138 L Paul Silverman/Fundamental Photographs
139 T Jeff Greenberg/Visuals Unlimited
139 B Lawrence Migdale/Photo Researchers
143 T Breck P. Kent/Animals Animals/Earth Scenes
143 B Renee Lynn/Photo Researchers
145 Kim Westerskov/Tony Stone Images
146 Oliver Benn/Tony Stone Images
147 NASA/SS/Photo Researchers
148 Ulrike Welsch/Photo Researchers
149 B Sylvain Grandadam/Photo Researchers
150 Background PhotoDisc, Inc.
150 TC Phil McCarten/PhotoEdit
150 CR Corel
150 BL MetaTools
151 TL PhotoDisc, Inc.
151 T David Young-Wolff/Tony Stone Images
155 Renee Lynn/Photo Researchers
157 UPI/Corbis-Bettmann
159 T PhotoDisc

Unit C
1 Merrilee Thomas/TOM STACK & ASSOCIATES
2 T Vincent O'Bryne/Panoramic Images
2 BL A. Gragera/Latin Stock/SPL/Photo Researchers
2 C Merrilee Thomas/TOM STACK & ASSOCIATES
3 C NASA
3 B Geoff Tompkinson/SPL/Photo Researchers
4 Inset NOAA/TOM STACK & ASSOCIATES
9 T Stephen Ferry/Liaison Agency
9 B NOAA/TOM STACK & ASSOCIATES
13 Gary W. Carter/Visuals Unlimited
15 BL Bayard H. Brattstrom/Visuals Unlimited
15 TR Robert Stahl/Tony Stone Images
15 TL A. J. Copley/Visuals Unlimited
15 BR Lincoln Nutting/Photo Researchers
17 Frank Oberle/Tony Stone Images
18 The Newberry Library/Stock Montage
19 Granger Collection
20 C Christian Grzimek/Okapia/Photo Researchers
20 Background PhotoDisc, Inc.
21 T Dr. E. R. Degginger/Color-Pic, Inc.
21 Background PhotoDisc
22 B Joyce Photographics/Photo Researchers
22 T Davis Instruments
23 Howard Bluestein/Photo Researchers
24 B David Parker/ESA/SPL/Photo Researchers
24 T TSADO/NCDC/NASA/TOM STACK & ASSOCIATES
25 T TSADO/NCDC/NASA/TOM STACK & ASSOCIATES"
30 Courtesy of NOAA Photo Library
32 Charles Doswell III/Tony Stone Images
34 Wetmore/Photo Researchers
35 T Alan R. Moller/Tony Stone Images
35 B Dan McCoy/Rainbow
36 L NASA/SPL/Photo Researchers
36 R R. Perron/Visuals Unlimited
37 Alan R. Moller/Tony Stone Images
39 T SADO/NCDC/NASA/TOM STACK & ASSOCIATES
46 L Francois Gohier/SSC/Photo Researchers